5 minutes

TO A GREAT

REAL ESTATE

SALES MEETING

JOHN D. MAYFIELD

ABR®, ABRM, GRI, e-PRO®, CRB

THOMSON

SOUTH-WESTERN™

Australia · Canada · Mexico · Singapore · Spain · United Kingdom · United States

THOMSON
™
SOUTH-WESTERN

5 Minutes to a Great Real Estate Sales Meeting

John D. Mayfield

VP/Editorial Director:
Jack W. Calhoun

VP/Editor-in-Chief:
Dave Shaut

Senior Publisher:
Karen Schmohe

Acquisitions Editor:
Scott Person

Developmental Editor:
Jennifer Warner

Marketing Manager:
Mark Linton

Production Editor:
Cliff Kallemeyn

Manufacturing Coordinator:
Charlene Taylor

Media Editor:
Rhonda Brown

Design Project Manager:
Rik Moore

**Production House/
Compositor:**
DPS Associates, Inc.

Printer:
West

I dedicate this book in memory of my dad, John Mayfield.
He taught me so much, and I will be forever appreciative
for his guidance, support, love, and friendship.

Contents

Forward

5 Minutes to a Great Real Estate Sales Meeting is a treasure chest of ideas for the real estate broker/manager. John Mayfield has created a simple and easy-to-use game plan for you to use week in and week out in preparing and running your real estate sales meetings.

One of the biggest obstacles we face as real estate sales office owners is the responsibility of educating our agents. This is an obligation that must not be taken lightly, and with education and training comes the need to hold effective, creative, and informative meetings for our agents. A great meeting will educate your agents and provide them the necessary tools they will need to succeed. As brokers and managers we should make certain those meetings can be the stepping stones to allowing agents to move further in their real estate careers. *5 Minutes to a Great Real Estate Sales Meeting* by John D. Mayfield will help you reach that objective.

I have personally worked with John through the Missouri Association of REALTORS®, and I can attest that John is an excellent educator and a very successful broker and owner.

Many of the meeting agendas included with this book have accompanying Microsoft® PowerPoint slide shows. If you are not using a projector and Microsoft® PowerPoint with your meetings, I strongly encourage you to do so. Statistics show that 80 percent of people learn visually and that visual presentations are much more successful in retention of knowledge. With John's help, and through *5 Minutes to a Great Real Estate Sales Meeting* you will find the added PowerPoint slides very beneficial in delivering a top-notch sales meeting.

I encourage you to use this book in a couple of ways. First, use the book to plan your sales meeting. While you are using the material and preparing for your meeting, ask yourself what additional issues your agents have experienced regarding the specific topic. Also, think about what additional questions you should ask to stimulate group discussion.

The second way to use this book is to write down new ideas as you prepare for your meeting. This will be the genesis of a meeting that you can present to your group in the near future.

Each meeting agenda is designed for you to use as it is, or you may delete items that do not apply, or add additional thoughts, as you deem necessary. Each sales meeting is a blank canvas to paint a picture of how you want your agents to see and understand the subject matter. Whatever way works best for you, incorporate that style into your sales meeting to give your agents a presentation they will not forget.

Best of all, with John's help, you're only *5 Minutes to a Great Real Estate Sales Meeting*!

Richard Mendenhall
President of the National Association of REALTORS®, 2001

Introduction

It's been a typical Monday and you finally leave the office after six o'clock. You hope to catch dinner with your family before leaving for your child's vocal concert at school. A million things from today's hectic day are screeching through your mind as you sit at the traffic light, which seems to have been red for hours. You look at the clock in your car and it's 6:25. There's at least another 15 minutes to get home, provided you don't run into any more problems. Suddenly it dawns on you that tomorrow is Tuesday, and you're not completely ready for your sales meeting in the morning. *How could things pile up like they do and pull you away from being ready for the biggest day of the week in front of your sales associates?* You think to yourself that by the time the choir concert is finished and you spend some quality time with your wife and children, it will be well after 10 o'clock. *How will you finish everything? How can you enjoy your child's big school event when you know all you will be thinking about is tomorrow's sales meeting?*

Another scenario could play out like this. You're managing a successful office and have plenty of assistance and time on your hands to prepare each week for your office meeting. Yet, while you look over your notes and realize it's time to cover Fair Housing laws again, you struggle to come up with something new. You need a fresh approach to grab your agents' attention and bring them back week after week. Still, you would love to incorporate some technology into your weekly meetings to give them a little pizzazz. How can you accomplish this?

Through *5 Minutes to a Great Real Estate Sales Meeting*, I will help provide a new approach to your sales meetings for the next year and beyond. In my own career, I watched each week come and go in what appeared to be the blink of an eye. I literally could be the person described in the first paragraph. Yes, I had good intentions of preparing for my upcoming sales meeting that Tuesday morning, but time was just not on my side. I found myself becoming discouraged by my lack of preparation and felt that in some way I was letting my agents down. Then one day it dawned on me—why not write a book that contains sales meeting templates that all brokers and managers can use for their weekly sales meetings? As I pondered the idea, it finally occurred to me just how many issues we need to cover in a year's time; everything from legal issues, such as fair housing and lead-based paint disclosures to motivating our agents and helping them make it through another day in this stressful business. And, lest we forget, prospecting! Our business is built on building and retaining clients! Group all of these topics together, as well as many more, such as learning today's technology, and you can begin to see the task at hand in preparing for weekly sales meetings. And yes, this is only a small portion of our job descriptions as brokers and managers.

5 Minutes to a Great Real Estate Sales Meeting is packed with timely issues and quick and easy sales meeting ideas that make a positive impression on your agents. Whether you have more than enough time each week to prepare, or if you fall into the role of the managing broker who finds his or her time stolen away each week with problems and issues, you will profit from owning this book. Most of the meeting topics contain quizzes and other related handouts that can be printed out to copy and distribute to your agents without a lot of work. I have also provided the material in two formats for you to use. If you own Microsoft® Word, you can open the quiz or handout and edit the text you choose to make the meeting personalized the way you would want it. If you do not own Microsoft® Word, the material is also saved in Acrobat PDF, which is free and available to anyone by downloading the Acrobat Reader software at http://www.adobe.com. Many meetings have accompanying slide shows on the resource CD. All slide shows use Microsoft® PowerPoint, and are available for you to run from the resource CD. You will find the resource CD helpful in accomplishing your preparation to delivering a great sales meeting to your agents without a lot of work.

This book has also provided several extra tools to help you organize your year as a broker/manager. First, it will help you track your meetings throughout the year as to the type of meetings you offer and the date you offered each one. This guide will make sure that you are providing a good mix of meeting topics for your agents. It will also provide an excellent resource if you should happen to be audited by your local or state real estate governing body. By tracking your meetings you can show the steps you took to train and educate your agents.

Many of the meeting topics are given from an alternate angle or approach. Agents expect and want something different, and not the same old resources thrown at them, sometimes year after year. With *5 Minutes to a Great Real Estate Sales Meeting*, you can rest assured that the material you provide will be a fresh and innovative approach to timely subjects they need to learn about. Each chapter provides a list of items to conduct the sales meeting and a list of meeting objectives. Most of the meetings are designed to last from 15 to 20 minutes. However, the goal of the book is for you to take a meeting and add or subtract from the meeting to fit your style and time frame. Even though the plan might indicate that the lesson is 15 to 20 minutes in length, you can generally figure that the meeting will go much longer, especially if you have good discussion from your agents.

Finally, the material is designed to be used either in its present form, or edited so you can approach it from your own perspective. I realize that everything I say will not fit your style or approach, but hopefully I can help stir the creative juices in your own mind so you can add your own personal flavor to each meeting as you choose. Each PowerPoint slide show or handout is fully editable for you to customize the presentation to your liking.

So how will you handle your next sales meeting preparation nightmare? It's easy, read on and discover!

Acknowledgements

Thank you to my mother, Pat Mayfield, who introduced me to the field of real estate at the age of 18. I have always said Mom taught me everything I needed to know about real estate.

I would also like to say thank you to all of my agents and staff at Mayfield Real Estate. You are the best group of real estate agents a broker could ask for. Special thanks to Zac McDowell for all of your hard work and honest opinions. Thanks to Susie McBride, my assistant, for all of her hard work in helping me get the book in its final form, and adding a special touch to the many handouts and forms included on the resource CD.

Thanks to Digital Juice and Presentation Pro for their Power Point backgrounds, and to Crystal Graphics for the closing quotes to each sales meeting. I would also like to thank the Washington Association of REALTORS® for the use of their safety material, the Department of HUD, and the EPA for additional information from their web sites.

Thank you to Richard Mendenhall, and to Kay Gerken, Elizabeth Mendenhall, Jim Asbury, Steve Snook, Mark Nash, and Jim Bolin, my reviewers, for their great suggestions for the book.

Thank you to Jennifer Warner, my editor. I was so fortunate to have such a wonderful person assist me on this project and to listen when I had questions and concerns.

Thank you to my two daughters, Alyx and Anne. Thanks for allowing Dad to spend so much time on this project.

And finally, thanks to my wonderful wife, Kerry. You always allow and encourage me to reach for the stars. I am so grateful to have you for my wife. You're the best!

Other Essential Real Estate Resources from South-Western:

Jacobus/Olmos	*Real Estate Dictionary: A Pocket Guide for Professionals*	032420518X
Lyon	*Instant Tax Relief for Real Estate Agents*	0324201435
Nash	*Starting & Succeeding in Real Estate*	0324224044
Herd	*Real Estate Office Management: A Guide to Success*	0324184840
Herd	*How to Become a Mega-Producer Real Estate Agent in 5 Years*	0324207476
Kennedy/Jamison	*How to List & Sell Real Estate*	0324188692
Kennedy	*Seven Figure Selling*	0324187513

For more information about South-Western's professional development and other real estate materials, visit us at http://www.realestate.swcollege.com Or call 1-800-354-9706.

Motivational Meetings

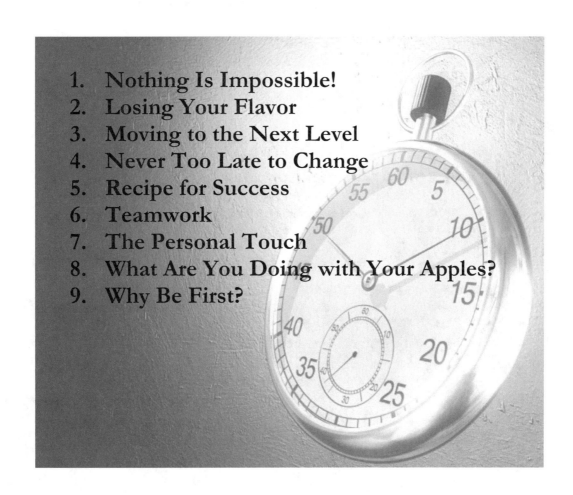

Nothing Is Impossible!

Theme: Motivating Agents to Believe in Themselves

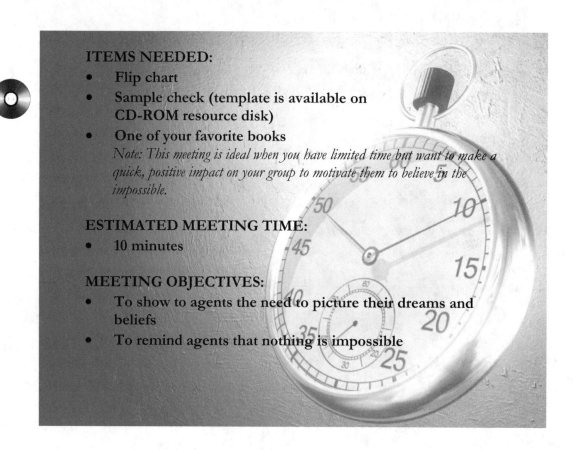

ITEMS NEEDED:
- Flip chart
- Sample check (template is available on CD-ROM resource disk)
- One of your favorite books
  Note: This meeting is ideal when you have limited time but want to make a quick, positive impact on your group to motivate them to believe in the impossible.

ESTIMATED MEETING TIME:
- 10 minutes

MEETING OBJECTIVES:
- To show to agents the need to picture their dreams and beliefs
- To remind agents that nothing is impossible

MEETING APPLICATION:

Step 1

Ask agents the following questions:

- If you could have anything you wanted right now, what would it be?
- If you could travel anywhere you wanted, where would you go?
- If you had a million dollars to give to a charitable organization, to whom would you write your check?
- How do you plan on realizing your dreams?

Step 2

Have the agents take out a personal check (if they have their checkbooks with them) and write out a check to themselves for the amount they dream of earning some year. (Be sure to have the agents write "Void" on the signature line area to avoid possible security problems.) If there are agents who do not have their checkbooks with them, use the sample check template from the resource CD to print out in advance for agents to use. Tell each agent to carry this check in his or her wallet or purse and look at it often as a reminder of the need to believe that he or she can one day, indeed, cash this check. As simple as this exercise is, it will come true if each one will only believe!

Step 3

Hold up the book you brought to the sales meeting. Ask the group the following questions:

- If you read this book on a daily basis, would you complete the reading someday?
  Naturally the answer is "yes."
- If you re-read this book over and over, would you begin to memorize portions of the book?
  Again, the answer is "yes."

Remind agents that the same is true for our goals and dreams. We must remind ourselves each day what our wants and desires are, and one way to do this is by reading our goals daily.

Step 4

Hold up the sample check you prepared in advance. Encourage the group to take out the checks they wrote to themselves earlier in the meeting and read them again. Encourage them to look, touch, and read their checks every day.

Tell the agents that they can cash their checks some day. All they have to do is believe!

Finish the Sales Meeting With This Quote:

"To be a great champion you must believe you are the best. If you're not, pretend you are."
Muhammad Ali

ADDITONAL NOTES TO COVER DURING MEETING

MOTIVATIONAL
MEETING

2

Losing Your Flavor

THEME: Helping Agents Avoid Burn-Out

ITEMS NEEDED:
- Candle and matches
- Flavored gum packet with an assortment of flavors placed inside a large plastic bag
- Flip chart
- Personal Assessment Evaluation handout from resource CD
- Blank current month's or next month's calendar for each agent

ESTIMATED MEETING TIME:
- 15 minutes

MEETING OBJECTIVES:
- To help agents learn how to keep from becoming stale in the real estate business
- To help agents learn how to avoid burn-out

MEETING APPLICATION:

Step 1

Write the following on the flip chart:

Areas of Concern

1. Burn-Out
2. Loss of Joy

Tell the group that today's meeting deals with avoiding burn-out.

Step 2

Hand out the chewing gum, and ask those who would like to chew the gum during this meeting as an experiment to do so. Provide agents with the Personal Assessment Evaluation (below, and available on the resource CD) and allow them time to complete the handout.

Personal Assessment Evaluation

Answer the questions below. Be honest, and think about each question before you try to answer.

1. List one item that you dread doing daily in your real estate career.

2. Now, reflect on your entire daily schedule. What do you do regularly at work? List as many repeated items as you can.

3. Do you have a regularly scheduled day off from work? If yes, what day or days do you rest?

4. Do you have a personal assistant helping you?

5. If no, why?

6. If yes, do you delegate enough responsibilities to your assistant? List any other items you could assign to your assistant.

7. List one item that you could delegate to someone else that would make you enjoy your career again.

Step 3

Ask the following questions before reviewing the Personal Assessment Evaluation, and have the agents decide what the answers might be.

- During a car race, a big puff of smoke suddenly pours out from a car's hood. What do you think happened? *The engine blew up? Maybe it ran out of oil?*

- You place a hot iron on top of fabric and it sticks to the material. What is likely wrong with the iron? *It is out of water and could produce no steam.*

- You chew the same stick of gum for over six hours. What has happened to the gum? *It lost its flavor a long time ago.*

- A candle that burns continuously will normally do what? *Burn out!*

Explain to the group that no matter who you are, or what you're made of, at some time, if you are not careful, you will burn out. The four analogies above clearly show that engines need oil to run correctly, an iron needs steam, chewing gum, no matter how good, will lose its flavor after time, and candles will eventually burn out.

Step 4

Review the personal assessment with the agents, and explain in advance that one way to avoid burn-out is to discover a little bit about ourselves and what we are doing each day. Suggest to agents that maybe it's time to hire a personal assistant, delegate other work to someone, or hire a new agent in the office to help with transactions, and help train new agents in their careers. Of course, for any agent to avoid burn-out, he or she must learn to take some time off. Go through each question with your group and ask for the group to suggest ways to handle each topic. Allow those who want to volunteer their responses to do so, but explain that this assessment is for their information and it is not necessary to share it with the group.

Step 5

Pass out the monthly calendar you copied in advance. Ask each agent present to look at the next thirty days and determine or schedule some time off from work. Encourage agents to mark off time to spend with their families and friends. This is a good time to remind agents that it is essential to schedule time off on a monthly, quarterly, and even an annual basis.

Have agents make a list of all the tasks and to do's on their agendas for today and the coming week. Ask the agents to place asterisks next to those items that they would like to assign to someone else to take care of. Tell them you will come back to this list at the conclusion of the meeting.

Step 6

Hold up a new stick of chewing gum. Ask those who are chewing if the gum has already lost its flavor. Even if it hasn't, would they want to chew this gum all day long? At some point it will lose its flavor and the gum will be useless to them. Then, they will want to spit it into the wastebasket and try a new flavor. The neat part about our business is that if we get tired of doing the same old work, we can get rid of the job we dislike and replace it with something else. Encourage agents to delegate work that has lost its excitement, or find new ways to improve their attitudes toward these tasks. Make the point that switching flavors can help the agents' longevity in the real estate business as well.

Step 7

The final point to drive home to the group is about burn-out. Light the candle in front of the group. Explain that this candle looks large and could burn for hours, but eventually it will burn out. Our real estate careers are in danger of the same problem if we are not careful. One way we can keep our batteries recharged and our candles burning longer is by delegating repeated or tedious tasks we do not enjoy. We can also avoid burn-out by scheduling time off for ourselves each month.

Have agents look back over their lists of things to do today and during the upcoming week, and have them develop a plan to relieve some of the issues that are bogging them down. Insist that agents plan the next thirty days of their schedules and arrange to take some time off. Remind agents that if they do not take this sales meeting seriously and avoid the topics covered, they are in danger of burning out at some point in the future. Blow out the candle during the last statement to drive home your point with a good visual effect.

Finish the Sales Meeting With This Quote:

> *"To be able to look back on one's past life with satisfaction is to live twice."* Marcus Valerius Martialis 'Martial' (c.40 A.D.–102 A.D.) Roman epigrammatist, poet, friend of Juvenal

ADDITONAL NOTES TO COVER DURING MEETING

MOTIVATIONAL MEETING

3

Moving to the Next Level

THEME: Helping Agents Climb the Real Estate Ladder to Success

ITEMS NEEDED:
- Small or regular size ladder, with strips of colored paper taped to each step
  Strips are located on the resource CD for you to print and cut out. In place of the ladder you could use a side wall in your meeting room as shown under Step 2.
- A thick-tipped marker to write on the paper
- Flip chart

ESTIMATED MEETING TIME:
- 10–15 minutes

MEETING OBJECTIVES:
- To encourage agents to discover at what stage they are in their real estate careers, and to brainstorm how they can move up to the next level
- To remind top agents of the need to refocus their current work plans and develop new ways of doing real estate so that they, too, can increase their business and avoid losing market share to others climbing the ladder

MEETING APPLICATION:

Step 1

In advance, affix strips of paper to the steps on your ladder so the words on them are visible to the group. The top of the ladder should have a strip with the word "#1" written on it. The next step down from the top should have a strip of paper with the words "Missing 1 Ingredient." The next step down should read "Mind-set." The step below that will read "Your Perception/Branding." For the remaining steps place strips with the following words in order, or, when you get the bottom step, tape all the words on this step. On the bottom step, be sure you can pull the strips off one at a time without disturbing the previous strip of paper. The words should be in this order:

- Education
- Knowledge
- Commitment
- Time
- Prospecting
- Support
- Financial Means
- Experience
- Enjoyment

Step 2

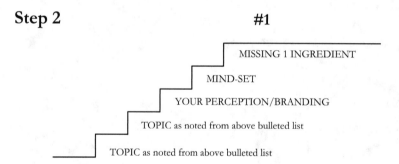

#1

MISSING 1 INGREDIENT

MIND-SET

YOUR PERCEPTION/BRANDING

TOPIC as noted from above bulleted list

TOPIC as noted from above bulleted list

Step 3

Using the ladder or the wall with the strips of paper attached for your visual, begin to discuss the progression of the typical real estate agent in our business. Discuss the bottom pool or lowest rung of the ladder and the various issues that many real estate agents face. Unfortunately, many real estate agents will never make it to the first level of progression. Talk about the topics that tend to frustrate or block the growth of the new agent.

- Knowledge and education are essential for anyone to advance in our industry. As Joseph Addison stated, *"Knowledge is that which, next to virtue, truly raises one person above another."*
- Time and commitment are factors that prevent some agents from moving to the next level. If agents are not willing to invest the time and commitment, they will never succeed in real estate.

- For some it might be the issue of prospecting. Without prospecting the growth of clients will be limited and the agent will become discouraged and leave the business.
- Real estate agents need support to prosper and move on to the next level. Support both from their families and from the office is essential. Discuss ways your office provides support to the agents. If you need to improve your own inner-office support system, this is a good time to make your new commitments.
- Financial means can sometimes drive good potential agents from succeeding in our industry. Unfortunately, the commission-based structure will eliminate those who cannot survive the initial costs and length of time required to build a business.
- Experience is always an ingredient to help agents move to the next level. Planting good solid roots will help an agent ride out the storm during a long drought of business. Experience helps!
- Enjoyment. Many agents will never make it out of the gate because real estate is not what they like.

Ask the group if they have any other thoughts on why some real estate agents never get off the first step.

Step 4

Now discuss the following steps in their listed order.

- *Your Perception/Branding.* Point out to the agents that those who want to break out of the "average" real estate agent mode must set themselves apart from the competition. In other words, their friends and others in their marketplace must associate real estate with them. Ask the group for some suggestions on how to do this. *Note to the manager: If you have recently covered the sales meeting on branding, encourage the group to think back on some of the ideas generated from that meeting.*

- *Mind-set.* Advise the agents that as we move farther and farther up the ladder, the number of agents in this group becomes smaller and smaller. Many agents cannot visualize themselves in the higher percentage of top agents in the board. Anyone wanting to advance to that higher level must believe in himself or herself. Sports provides a good example of this. There are many professional athletes, but we really remember only a small portion of them. Michael Jordon, Jack Nicklaus, and Tiger Woods are all good examples of athletes who have openly voiced their ability to picture positive results. Good real estate agents believe in themselves and have the right mind-set. Ask for suggestions on how a person can develop the right mind-set. *One way is to write your goals down and look at them every day!* (Refer to the meeting on "Believe" if previously covered.)

- *Missing 1 Ingredient.* As you point to the next-to-the-top level, explain to the group that probably the only difference between the agent who is #1 and the agents who fall into the next level is one ingredient. Perhaps this group relies too heavily on past business and needs to prospect more. Maybe their branding or image is not right in front of the community and is therefore not drawing in new business. Maybe there are agents in this group who are swamped with too much work and who need to hire assistants, or maybe it's time to add additional staff to the team. Perhaps its time to learn how to implement a team approach or use an assistant more effectively.

Whatever the problem is, the agents in this category need to take a good healthy evaluation of themselves and/or their teams, and ask what it is that will rejuvenate their business and jump-start them to the top position. Encourage agents to meet with you for a brainstorming session to discover what their missing ingredient might be.

- *#1.* As you point to the top step on the ladder (#1), you must remind the group that whenever a person or a team makes it to the top, they cannot let up or relax, because as much work as it took to make it there, the same amount of knowledge will be required to stay there. The only difference is that now the procedures and methods are in place.

Step 5

This is a good time to encourage the agents to meet with you on self-evaluations. Make a note of the fact that "everyone started at the beginning" to encourage the newer agents.

Ask the group the following questions. Encourage the agents to think about these issues, and not to respond verbally:

- Where do you feel you are on the real estate ladder?
- Can you do better than you are currently doing?
- What obstacles stand in your way, keeping you from making it further up the ladder?
- What actions can you take to help?
- Who can make it to the top step? *ANYONE!*

Again, this would be an excellent time to set appointments with agents to perform evaluations and brainstorming sessions about their real estate careers.

Finish The Sales Meeting With This Quote:

> *"The greatest pleasure in life is doing what people say you cannot do."* Walter Bagehot (1826–1877) English social scientist & literary critic, editor of *The Economist*

ADDITIONAL NOTES TO COVER DURING MEETING

Never Too Late to Change

THEME: Encouraging Agents to Realize that Each Day Has the Potential to Start a New Chapter in Their Lives

ITEMS NEEDED:

- Handout from resource CD
- 3 x 5 index cards
- Flip chart
- Small cake from bakery—place candles on the cake and light the candles

ESTIMATED MEETING TIME:

- 15–20 minutes

MEETING OBJECTIVE:

- To encourage agents to develop the necessary principles for moving forward and to realize it is never too late to change old habits

MEETING APPLICATION:

Step 1

Begin the meeting by asking for a volunteer to come forward and blow out the candles on the cake. Someone who has a birthday coming up or who just had a birthday would be ideal. Before the volunteer blows out the candles, ask the group what they would normally say had this been a real birthday: "Make a wish." Explain that for many people, as their lives move forward, they are always in a "wish" mode. "*I wish* I could have done this better or differently." "*I wish* I could incorporate this into my sales career." "*I wish* I could do that." These are all wishes that never get off the ground.

Step 2

Provide the handout from the CD and have agents answer the listed questions.

- What is the one thing you enjoy the most about this job?
- What are your positive qualities as a real estate agent?
- What is the one thing you dislike about selling real estate?
- What real estate areas do you feel you are weak in?
- Can you change the above answer? If so, how? Is real estate a career to you or do you look at it as simply a job?
- In your mind, what is the perfect day?
- If you could change anything about your real estate career, what would it be?
- If you could change anything about your life, what would it be?
- Think of the following: You are no longer in the real estate business, and one of your past clients walks into your former real estate office and asks for you. The agent at the desk explains that you are no longer in the real estate business. What positive qualities would you want your former client to say about you to the new agent at the front desk?
- Imagine that you have retired from a long and prosperous real estate career. The new broker/manager asks you to come and talk to the sales agents at one of their meetings. You know none of the agents present, although perhaps maybe a handful were just starting out when you retired. What would you tell them had helped you most in your real estate career?
- What other words would you leave the group with?

Step 3

After the group finishes their questions (which may take a few minutes) have them review their lists. Give the group blank index cards and have them use them to write out personal mission statements using the information from the answered questions. Direct the group to look at what their answers were, and see if they can find any underlying core principles to their answers. For example, what do they like most about their job, and what do they consider themselves good at? This should also line up with what advice they might give to new agents when they retire. Remind the agents that this exercise might not be easy, but it is important for them to discover what their mission statements are in life. Even though some may not have written a mission statement that they can look at day in and day out, it is essential. If they need help or want to discuss this with other agents, allow them the opportunity. Encourage everyone to create a mission statement and to write down what they feel their mission in life is all about.

Step 4

Ask the group the following questions:
- What does a mission statement have to do with your life?
- What are core values?
- What do your core values have to do with your mission statement?
- Why should your core values and your mission statement agree with each other?
- Would it be easier to perform a task if it were something you believed in?

Tell the group that sometimes we can get out of focus with our lives and not know it. Having a mission statement written down can keep us on track to what it is we want to accomplish in life. Building this mission around what is important to us is critical, as it becomes the glue that keeps everything together.

Step 5

Explain to the group that if there are areas of their real estate career or their personal lives that they feel frustrated with, it's never too late to change. Share the following story as mentioned from Glenn Van Ekeren's book, *Speaker's Sourcebook II*, Prentice Hall Press: *It's said that in the northlands of Canada there are only two seasons, a winter season and the month of July. The lands become so wet and soggy in July that as trucks and other vehicles travel through the countryside they leave deep ruts. When winter arrives again, the ruts freeze and make the roadways very treacherous. As vehicles approach these road areas it is said that there is a sign that reads, "Be careful of the rut you choose, as you will be in it for the next 20 miles." The same is true for our lives. We should be careful which way our lives lead, as we could end up in the same rut for many years to follow.*

Ask the group: "Is it too late to change?" *Never!*

Encourage agents to review their mission statements over the next few weeks, and to use their mission statements when planning their goals.

Step 6

Light the candles on top of the cake again. Ask the following questions:

- Do you still want to just make a wish?
- Are you ready to make that wish come true?

The choice is up to you because it is never too late to change!

Finish The Sales Meeting With This Quote:

> *"We progress because we are willing to change."* Thomas J. Watson
> (1874–1956) founder, chairman, and president of IBM. Thomas J. Watson in
> "Men–Minutes–Money, a Collection of Excerpts from Talks . . ."

ADDITIONAL NOTES TO COVER DURING MEETING

MOTIVATIONAL
MEETING

5

Recipe for Success

**THEME: Showing Agents that Success in Real Estate Is
Composed of a Multitude of Selling Ingredients**

ITEMS NEEDED:
- Flip chart
- Copies of various recipes from a cookbook or from an internet web site
- Handout from resource CD

ESTIMATED MEETING TIME:
- 10–15 minutes

MEETING OBJECTIVES:
- To show agents how becoming successful in the real estate industry takes a multitude of talents and endeavors
- To teach agents that leaving out just a few small ingredients can be detrimental to their success in the real estate industry
- To help agents develop a checklist of mutually agreed-upon objectives that will be developed by the group to show everyone what they feel represents a "recipe for success"

MEETING APPLICATION:

Step 1

In advance, write the following topics on a blank page of your flip chart:

- Dress
- Education (real-estate related)
- Prospecting
- Time Assigned
- Skills
- Miscellaneous

Begin the meeting by passing out copies of the recipes that you have chosen. Ask the agents to look over the recipes for a moment and highlight or make note of some of the ingredients. After allowing the agents a few moments to scan over their assigned recipes, ask for volunteers to share the title of their recipes with the group.

- Ask the volunteers if they have all the necessary ingredients to make this meal in their kitchens right now.
- Ask what steps they would have to take to make the recipes.
- Ask about the preparation time for their recipes.
- Ask what would happen if they left out one or two of the key ingredients in one of the recipes.
- Is it okay to be creative and add items to a recipe?
- Ask for more volunteers as you see fit and go back through the same questions.

Step 2

Referring to the flip chart, ask the group to focus their attention on the real estate industry and what "ingredients" they feel would go into a recipe for success. As the group responds, write their responses on the flip chart in each related area. You could also allow the group to divide into smaller groups and brainstorm these areas to develop a recipe for success that real estate agents could follow to be more productive.

Step 3

Ask the group these questions:

- What is success?
- Is success always tied to financial measures?
- Do you think there are some key ingredients to becoming successful in the real estate industry?
- Will every recipe work the same for every agent in becoming successful in the real estate industry?

Step 4 (Optional)

Distribute the template from the resource CD entitled "My Recipe for Success." Encourage agents to complete the recipe template from the ideas generated from the sales meeting and to carry it with them to review over the next few days or weeks.

Step 5

Briefly, tell the story of how Mrs. Fields Cookies came about. Debbi Sivyer Fields had a passion for cookies and enjoyed making them. She worked and worked to make her cookies perfect. In an interview for *Right on the Money*, Mrs. Fields said that "The cookies 20-plus years ago were small, crispy, and crunchy. In fact, they stated that that's what Americans liked in chocolate chip cookies. And for me, I loved them soft and chewy and fresh out of the oven, just laden with chocolate chips and great ingredients like butter." Mrs. Fields goes on to say later in the article that "Mrs. Fields was never a business. It was a part of me. It was an extension of me … I was never 9-to-5. And I never separated, oh, well, business from personal because to me they're all blended together. And, yes, it is all-consuming, but what matters is how you manage your priorities."

Explain to the agents that, like Debbi Sivyer Fields, their priority should be to have a passion for the real estate business. Without passion, successes in this career may be few and far between. They also need the right ingredients. Take away one item, and you have a different cookie. The same is true with real estate. You now have a good start to a recipe for success. Now go out and perfect it!

Finish the Sales Meeting With This Quote:

"I do not know anyone who has got to the top without hard work. That is the recipe. It will not always get you to the top, but should get you pretty near." Margaret Hilda Thatcher (1925–) British prime minister, 1979–1990 (longest tenure in 20th century, Europe's first female Prime Minister)

ADDITIONAL NOTES TO COVER DURING THIS MEETING

MOTIVATIONAL MEETING

6

Teamwork

THEME: Reminding the Group that When We Work as a Team, Everyone Will Win

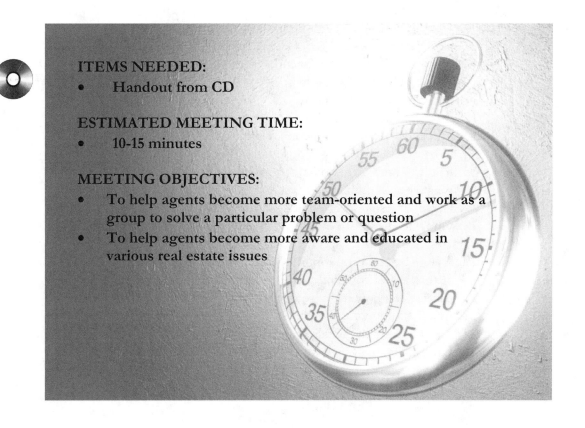

ITEMS NEEDED:
- Handout from CD

ESTIMATED MEETING TIME:
- 10-15 minutes

MEETING OBJECTIVES:
- To help agents become more team-oriented and work as a group to solve a particular problem or question
- To help agents become more aware and educated in various real estate issues

MEETING APPLICATION:

Step 1

Split agents up into groups of five or six, if possible. Print out the handout from the CD that includes the various questions. Explain to the group that they will be answering questions provided to them. Have groups work together to answer their questions. After they have finished, allow each group to exchange their answer sheets with another group and go over the quiz while each group scores the results. The team with the most correct answers at the end of the round wins. Record the results on a flip chart and provide a small prize for the winning team.

Questions for Teams

1. What was the name of Stephen King's first novel?
2. Who won the 1992 Super Bowl?
3. How many parties are involved in a deed of trust?
4. The promissory note serves what purpose in a real estate transaction?
5. Name the four unities in a joint tenancy.
6. Who served as the United States' third president?
7. What was the 47th state to join the United States?
8. How many wives did King Henry the VIII have?
9. What does the term "crescendo" mean?
10. In golf, what is a "scratch" handicap?
11. A football quarter has how many minutes?
12. A basketball half has how many minutes?
13. A hockey period has how many minutes?
14. In baseball, what goes in this blank? "the _____ inning stretch"
15. In a lease, the owner of the property is referred to as the _____.
16. What year were the Olympics last held in Los Angeles?
17. How many states begin with the letter "M"?
18. Who was the 2001 National Association of REALTORS® president?
19. A large pizza from Dominos® Pizza is how many inches in diameter, and contains approximately how many slices?
20. An acre has how many square feet?
21. A mile has how many feet?
22. A gallon of milk contains how many ounces?
23. What is the longest-running Broadway play?
24. Liens are considered to run with what?
25. Under IRS rules, land does not do what?

After agents have had some time to complete the quiz, go over the answers:

Questions for Teams

1. What was the name of Stephen King's first novel? *Carrie*
2. Who won the 1992 Super Bowl? *Washington Redskins*
3. How many parties are involved in a deed of trust? *3*
4. The promissory note serves what purpose in a real estate transaction? *the financing instrument*
5. Name the four unities in a joint tenancy. *"PITT:" Possession, Interest, Time, and Title*
6. Who served as the United States' third president? *Thomas Jefferson*
7. What was the 47th state to join the United States? *New Mexico*
8. How many wives did King Henry the VIII have? *6 wives*
9. What does the term "crescendo" mean? *Starting soft and then building to a louder sound.*
10. In golf, what is a "scratch" handicap? *even par*
11. A football quarter has how many minutes? *15*
12. A basketball half has how many minutes? *30*
13. A hockey period has how many minutes? *20*
14. In baseball, what goes in this blank? "the _____ inning stretch" *7th*
15. In a lease, the owner of the property is referred to as the _____. *lessor*
16. What year were the Olympics last held in Los Angeles? *1984*
17. How many states begin with the letter "M"? *8*
18. Who was the 2001 National Association of REALTORS® president? *Richard Mendenhall*
19. A large pizza from Dominos® Pizza is how many inches in diameter, and contains approximately how many slices? *14" and 8 slices*
20. An acre has how many square feet? *43,560*
21. A mile has how many feet? *5,280*
22. A gallon of milk contains how many ounces? *128*
23. What is the longest-running Broadway play? *Cats, 7485 performances*
24. Liens are considered to run with what? *Land*
25. Under the IRS rules, land does not do what? *Depreciate*

Step 2

Tally up the scores and give the prize to the group with the most correct answers. Explain to the group that the purpose of the exercise was to demonstrate the need and ability to work as a team. The questions cover a wide variety of topics. Some topics are weak areas of study for some individuals, while other people know a lot about them. Explain that this is what makes good teamwork. Everyone on the team has a trait or an ability to lend to the team. Where one is weak in an area another team player is strong. If we learn to utilize the concept of teamwork it can be a powerful tool. Stress that the key to effective teamwork is making sure everyone is included and involved on the team!

Step 3

Write "Team" on your flip chart to use as an acronym. Explain that an effective team can be thought of as the following, and go over the following points:

> **T = Togetherness.** The group must work as one unit and be *together* regardless of the situation. Whenever team players begin to work on their own, or fail to pass the ball to another team player, the team will break down.
>
> **E = Encouragement.** Teams must remember that everyone needs *encouragement* from time to time. Good team players realize the importance of encouraging other team players when they are down and need a boost. Encouraging those on the team by commenting on their positive attributes and helping them reach a little further with their careers can be a tremendous boost for the team.
>
> **A = Attitude.** Team players must have a positive *attitude* about working as a team and a good attitude about their team players. Having the wrong attitude will destroy a team in no time at all.
>
> **M = Marriage.** An effective team looks at the team as a *marriage*. Like any marriage, team players must be loyal to one another. The team that can function as a unit, and does not separate, will do great things.

Step 4

Remind the group that when we work as a team, everyone will win. Tell the group that there has never been a Super Bowl won by an individual person. Never has the Stanley Cup in hockey been given to one person. The same is true for the World Series, the NBA championship, and on and on. All of these awards for first place are given to the team. The groups that win these awards do so because they learned to win **as a team**. Encourage your group to do the same. Remember, there is no "I" in "Team"!

Finish the Sales Meeting With This Quote:

"Finding good players is easy. Getting them to play as a team is another story." Casey Stengel, Major League Baseball manager

ADDITIONAL NOTES TO COVER DURING MEETING

The Personal Touch

THEME: Reminding Agents of the Importance of Following Up on a Personal Level with Past Clients and Customers

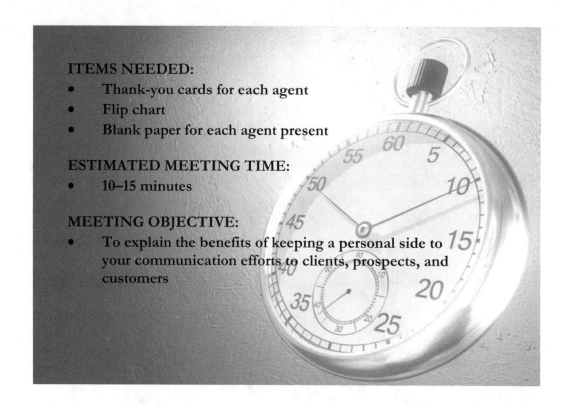

ITEMS NEEDED:
- Thank-you cards for each agent
- Flip chart
- Blank paper for each agent present

ESTIMATED MEETING TIME:
- 10–15 minutes

MEETING OBJECTIVE:
- To explain the benefits of keeping a personal side to your communication efforts to clients, prospects, and customers

MEETING APPLICATION:

Step 1

Pass out thank-you cards and blank paper to the agents. Have agents think of someone who has done something nice for them in the past week. (Any client who recently bought, sold, or re-listed a property with them is ideal.) If the agents have not sent thank-you cards for these actions, allow them a few minutes to do so now. If agents do not have mailing addresses readily available, tell them to address the envelopes with their return addresses and the names of the parties to receive the thank-you cards. They can finish addressing their cards after the meeting.

Step 2

Ask agents the following questions, and have them write their results on the blank paper you provided.

- What was the last major purchase you made in the last 12 months? Was it a car, boat, or other item of significant value?
- Did you receive any correspondence from the salesperson whom you dealt with?
- Did you receive a follow-up phone call from the sales associate?
- If you answered "yes," how many times have you heard from the salesperson since your purchase?
- Imagine that you just bought a home from a real estate professional. Would you want to hear from your salesperson after the sale?
- If yes, what type of communication should the agent provide?

Allow agents time to discuss this with you.

Step 3

Write the following acronym on your flip chart:

C   L   I   E   N   T

Have agents get into groups and allow them an opportunity to develop words that would go well with this acronym. You may use the following if your group has trouble developing a list of words. Post all responses on your flip chart.

Explain each letter below with the group:

> **C = Closeness.** In order for anyone to want you to represent him or her in a transaction, you must have some degree of *closeness*. Think of ways to encourage closeness with individuals. Staying in touch on a personal level can increase this level of closeness.
>
> continued…

L = Listening. It's surprising how much you will find out about someone by just *listening*. Often we will learn about interests, dreams, wants, and needs if we just listen to our clients. This brings to mind the quote, "Maybe this is why we have two ears and one mouth."

I = Interest. Have a unique *interest* in your clients' needs, and know what their areas of interest are. Sending articles on fly-fishing to a client who loves to fly fish will add a personal touch to your business and show clients you have an interest in them.

E = Empathy. Unless you have a desire and a care for your clients, you will never establish clients for life. People must know that you have *empathy* with them and their business in order for them to use you again and again.

N = Notes. Don't forget to send *notes* (handwritten) to your clients. Think back on any major purchase you made in the last 12 months. How impressed would you have been if your sales agent (or company) had sent you a handwritten note?

T = Touch. It is important to *touch* base with your clients (past and present) regularly. We can develop closeness with our clients and listen to their needs. We can have a unique interest in them, and know their interests. We can have a sincere empathy for our clients and send them notes once or twice, but if there is no continual "touching" base with them, we will eventually lose them to someone else. Why? Because someone else will begin a continuous stream of communication with them, and what was once our client will now belong to someone else.

Finish the Sales Meeting With This Quote:

"No student ever attains very eminent success by simply doing what is required of him; it is the amount and excellence of what is over and above the required, that determines the greatness of ultimate distinction."
Charles Kendall Adams

ADDITIONAL NOTES TO COVER DURING MEETING

What Are You Doing with Your Apples?

THEME: Demonstrating the Unlimited Possibilities that a Real Estate Career Can Offer

ITEMS NEEDED:
- An apple for each person in attendance
- Flip chart or some type of drawing board
  (You can have attendees jot down the group's responses on blank sheets of paper, if desired.)
- A rotten apple can be very effective, too, if you plan in advance

ESTIMATED MEETING TIME :
- 10–15 minutes

MEETING OBJECTIVES:
- To encourage agents to make the most out of their real estate careers
- To provide agents with a basic roadmap for making their real estate careers successful
- To remind agents of the endless possibilities as a real estate professional and the choices everyone has with regard to a career in real estate

MEETING APPLICATION:

Step 1

Make sure everyone in attendance receives a nice shiny apple. Next, ask the group to give you a list of things apples can be used for. Ideas such as apple pie, apple sauce, apple juice, apples in crafts, eating, etc. should come up. The list can become quite long. If you prefer, make your own list of things you can do with an apple. Write each response on the flip chart, and have fun discussing the various items brought up by the group.

Step 2

Next, explain to the group that their job is like an apple. They can do all kinds of things with their real estate careers if they just become creative. Pull out a copy of a real estate license and hold the paper up in front of your real estate agents. Explain that this license is their apple. They can make this apple do all kinds of things if they want to. They can hold open houses, hand out flyers, call "for-sale-by-owners," etc. The opportunities and ideas are limitless! Or, if they choose, they can do one more thing with this apple…let it just sit around and rot. (If you prepared for this in advance and have a rotten apple, you could reveal it at this point.)

Step 3

Write the following vertically on your flip chart: **A P P L E**

Alongside each letter finish the acronym as follows:

A = Attitude. We must have a good *attitude* to be successful in the real estate business. Our attitude will lead us to either be creative with our license or do nothing at all.

P = Plan. As real estate agents we must *plan* every day for how we will approach our business. Not only should we plan for the moment, but for our future as well. Encourage the group to set weekly, monthly, and yearly plans or goals.

P = Perform. A plan will do us no good unless we *perform*. Take your plans, execute them, and follow through so that performance will be automatic for each and every plan you put in place.

L = Look. *Look* outside the box for ways to increase your real estate career. (Remind your agents that, just as there have been many creative ideas as to how to use the apple, there are many new ways to do business as real estate professionals.)

continued…

E = Emulate. Agents who have had good luck in dealing with FSBO's or working the expired listings can be pointed out as being a good example to follow and *emulate* in those same areas. (This is a good opportunity to stroke the ego of those top producers in the office who enjoy recognition and praise in front of the group. Remind the agents to *emulate* others who have become successful with their real estate careers.)

Finish the Sales Meeting With This Quote:

> *"Some men never seem to grow old. Always active in thought, always ready to adopt new ideas, they are never chargeable with fogeyism. Satisfied, yet ever dissatisfied, settled, yet ever unsettled, they always enjoy the best of what is, are the first to find the best of what will be."* William Shakespeare (1564–1616)

ADDITONAL NOTES TO COVER DURING MEETING

MOTIVATIONAL MEETING

9

Why Be First?

THEME: Showing that Although Winning Is Not Everything, Having the Attitude and Mind-Set of a Winner Can Move Agents Closer to Their Goals

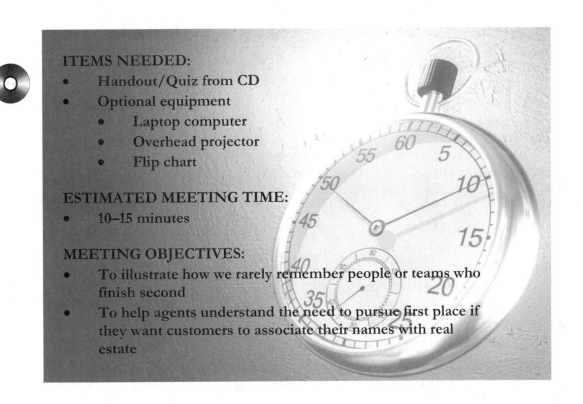

ITEMS NEEDED:
- Handout/Quiz from CD
- Optional equipment
    - Laptop computer
    - Overhead projector
    - Flip chart

ESTIMATED MEETING TIME:
- 10–15 minutes

MEETING OBJECTIVES:
- To illustrate how we rarely remember people or teams who finish second
- To help agents understand the need to pursue first place if they want customers to associate their names with real estate

MEETING APPLICATION:

Step 1

Have students complete the quiz, "Why Finish First?"

1. Who finished second in the Tour de France in 2002?
2. Who finished second in the Masters Golf Tournament in 2002?
3. What team lost the Super Bowl in 2003?
4. What team lost the World Series in 2002?
5. Who lost the presidential election in 1988?
6. Whom did Abraham Lincoln defeat in his bid for the presidency?
7. Whom did Franklin Roosevelt defeat in his bid for the presidency?
8. Whom did George Washington defeat in his bid for the presidency?
9. What movie won the Academy Award for best movie in 2003?
10. What were the other movies nominated for best movie in 2003?

After agents have had some time to complete the quiz, go over the answers:

1. Joseph Beloki
2. Retief Goosen
3. Oakland Raiders
4. New York Yankees
5. Michael Dukakis
6. Stephen Douglas, 1860
7. Herbert C. Hoover
8. John Adams
9. *Chicago*
10. *Gangs of New York, The Hours, The Lord of the Rings: The Two Towers, The Pianist*

Step 2

Ask the group the following questions:

- What is unique about finishing first?
- Why do most people want to finish first?
- Do most people remember who finishes in second place?
- Do most people remember who finished in first place?

Step 3

Write, in either a vertical or a horizontal position, the following acronym on your flip chart:

W I N N E R

Under or next to each letter write the following, and then use the explanation next to each word (or your own,) to describe what a winner is to your group.

- **W** ork
- **I** magination
- **N** ot
- **N** egative
- **E** nergetic
- **R** esilient

- **W = Work.** Almost all winners *work* hard. If you look at any athlete, team, or top sales associate in your office, they all have one common thread, and that is a great work ethic. There are countless hours of practice put into whatever their dream or goal is. We all remember Abraham Lincoln's famous quote about being able to fool some of the people all of the time, but not all of the people all of the time. Mr. Lincoln also said, *my father taught me to work; he did not teach me to love it.* Hard work is a necessity to being a "winner."

- **I = Imagination.** Having *imagination* is a fundamental principle of winners. If you cannot imagine yourself in the winners' circle then how can you really win? One of the key concepts that you hear over and over from athletes is how they visualize the golf shot being hit, how the basketball will go through the net, or pulling out ahead of the other competitors during the last 50 yard sprint. English editor and writer, Cyril Connolly, said that, "*imagination is nostalgia for the past, the absent; it is the liquid solution in which art develops the snapshot of reality.*" Have an imagination, and one that believes in you being a "winner!"

- **NN = Not Negative.** Combining the two "N"s forms the emphasis to stress to your agents that winners are *not negative*. The word *not* is never present in a winners mind! Winners must always turn the *negative* into a positive. They are always optimistic, and believe things will get better. Hank Aaron went 0 for 4 in his first professional baseball game. Had he let the negative thoughts of how he performed that first game affect him, he would have never gone on to become the homerun leader we know today.

continued...

- **E = Energetic.** Have you ever known of a winner who was not *energetic?* Working hard and being energetic go hand in hand. All winners spend hours and hours perfecting their game. Like successful athletes, real estate agents must work hard to develop a rewarding career. This will happen only with an energetic attitude. The famous American poet and author Ralph Waldo Emerson said "the world belongs to the energetic."

- **R = Resilient.** Winners are *resilient* in overcoming problems or setbacks. They don't let issues or losses get them down, and they are focused on the ultimate prize, "winning." Winners know how to make lemonade out of lemons! It was Vince Lombardi who said, "It's not whether you get knocked down. It's whether you get up again."

Step 4

Remind the group that although winning is not everything, having the attitude and mindset of a winner can move us closer to our goals. Besides that, "winning is just plain fun!"

Finally, encourage the group to remember that when the team wins, everyone wins.

Finish the Sales Meeting With This Quote:

"If winning isn't important, why keep score?" unknown

ADDITIONAL NOTES TO COVER DURING MEETING

Marketing Meetings

1. Branding Off-Line
2. Creating a Brand
3. Building Clients for Life
4. E-Newsletters Part I
5. E-Newsletters Part II
6. MLS® Signatures
7. Preparing Your Case
8. Direct Mail
9. Working with First-Time Buyers
10. Working with Senior Adults

MARKETING MEETING

1

Branding Off-Line

THEME: Marketing Yourself So Consumers Will Think of You When They Think of Real Estate

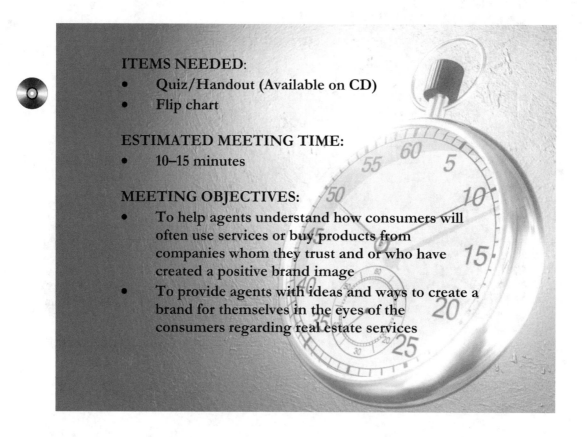

ITEMS NEEDED:
- Quiz/Handout (Available on CD)
- Flip chart

ESTIMATED MEETING TIME:
- 10–15 minutes

MEETING OBJECTIVES:
- To help agents understand how consumers will often use services or buy products from companies whom they trust and or who have created a positive brand image
- To provide agents with ideas and ways to create a brand for themselves in the eyes of the consumers regarding real estate services

MEETING APPLICATION:

Step 1

Have agents complete the exercise below:

> Write down the first word or words that come to mind:
>
> 1. Soap _____
> 2. Laundry detergent _____
> 3. Tissue paper _____
> 4. Facial tissue _____
> 5. Spaghetti sauce _____
> 6. Fast-food restaurant _____
> 7. Soda _____
> 8. Place you would call for pizza _____
> 9. Bank _____
> 10. Loan Officer _____
> 11. Real estate agent _____

Step 2

Ask agents what most of the words have in common.
Answer: A "brand" of awareness created in their minds.

Ask participants to share some of their answers and find out how many people had the same responses.

Focus on questions 8, 9, and 10. Ask for responses.

- Why did you choose these local businesses or individuals?

Write the responses on the flip chart.

Now focus on question 11, real estate agent.

- Did some of the agents list themselves? What were some of the responses when asked why?

Step 3

Have participants get into groups of two or three and brainstorm some ways that they could begin marketing themselves so that the public thinks of them when they think of real estate. List all the responses on the flip chart. This exercise should produce several good ideas that help agents realize what they should be doing but have, thus far, failed to do.

Some of these ideas may include

- Monthly newsletters
- Farming a subdivision
- Sending out congratulation notes
- Advertising (such as billboards)
- Newspaper advertisement
- Direct mail
- Holding open houses regularly
- Buying and selling seminars
- Providing excellent support service before, during, and after the sale

Step 4

Ask the following questions:

- What is the most important decision you must make in creating a brand for your real estate career?
- Why?
- Do you think a visual or photograph is important to creating a brand?
- Why or why not?
- How important do you think a "name" is when creating a brand?

Explain that according to Al and Laura Ries in their book, *The 22 Immutable Laws of Branding*, "The most important branding decision you will ever make is what to name your product and service."

Ask the group if they feel that advertising and branding are one and the same.

Rob Frankel, author of *The Revenge of Brand X*, explains in his ninth law of big time branding that "Advertising is not branding. Branding is branding. Advertising raises the awareness of the brand you create."

Step 5

Remind the agents that all the companies listed in the exercise started out with no one knowing who they were and what their products were about. It took a good product, hard work, and excellent customer service to build the trust and loyalty many of us now give back to them. As real estate agents, we are no different. We can earn that same loyalty and trust from our customers and clients if we use the right methods. Encourage the agents to be mindful of this in all of their actions, advertising, and hard work. Over time, this will create a "brand" awareness in consumers' minds so that people think of these agents when they think of real estate.

Finish the Sales Meeting With This Quote:

"Men of genius are admired, men of wealth are envied, men of power are feared; but only men of character are trusted." Alfred Adler (1870–1937) Austrian psychologist & psychiatrist

ADDITIONAL NOTES TO COVER DURING MEEETING

Creating a Brand

THEME: Marketing Yourself Online Through Today's Technology

ITEMS NEEDED:
- Flip chart
- Blank paper
- Optional equipment:
  - Laptop
  - Overhead projector
  - Access to the Internet

(If you do not have access to the Internet, print copies of the web sites in advance.)

ESTIMATED MEETING TIME:
- 10–15 minutes

MEETING OBJECTIVES:
- To help agents learn additional ways to market themselves online (via the Internet) to consumers and clients in their communities
- To examine ways that agents can promote their real estate services to potential clients moving into the area from other parts of the country or from outside the United States
- To allow agents to brainstorm ideas to include on their web sites

MEETING APPLICATION:

Step 1

If there is an agent in the office who has had success in creating a brand image (slogan or logo) in your real estate marketplace, allow that agent a few moments to talk about how beneficial it has been for his or her real estate business. Ask the agent to elaborate on how he or she came up with ideas. Next, have agents take their blank paper and use three to five minutes to write down everything they can think of that is unique, fun, outrageous, and memorable about themselves. Encourage agents to dig deep into their inner selves to list information individual to them and them alone in the marketplace. For example, if someone's name is different or unusual, write it down. Tell them to be creative and write whatever comes to mind regardless of what they might think about it; just write down every thought that passes through their minds in the next few minutes.

Step 2

Next, have the agents list everything they feel a strong desire for or belief about. What's important to them as individuals?

Step 3

The next step to discovering our online presence focuses on blending topics from the first and second categories. Ask agents to see if they can find a relationship or theme that might form from their two lists. (*Note:* This will be the harder step in our process and may require the group to spend a few more minutes on this topic.) For example, a person named Paul who has a strong work ethic might use the slogan, *"Paul Works Hard!"*

Step 4

Now have each agent pair up with another agent and exchange their papers. Have the groups look at the information written down and see if they can spot a phrase or slogan from the information put together. Remind the group to not laugh or make fun of any ideas written down by their team members. Allow the groups to discuss their lists together.

Step 5

After several minutes bring the groups back together and discuss any suggestions or ideas from groups willing to volunteer. Write the ideas on your flip chart. Title the flip chart "Online Branding."

Discussion Points
- Talk about each idea and ask the group to think of possible logos.
- Think of visuals that would work well with the slogans or brand names listed.
- Ask the group, "What would good give-aways be to promote your web site?" (Be careful to check your state license laws and rules and regulations to find out what is permissible before engaging in any free give-away).

- Then ask, "How could you advertise and promote your new web site to the community?"

Step 6

If you have a projector available visit the following web sites.

- http://www.PaulWorksHard.com
- http://www.DallasHomes.com
- http://www.Duckin.com
- http://www.MarkSellsStLouis.com
- http://www.MarieFarnsWorth.com
- http://www.ToniTygart.com
- http://www.RealAgent.net
- http://www.SharpHomesSell.com
- http://www.WendySanda.com

You might also consider visiting http://www.hobbsherder.com for more ideas and tips about online branding. Encourage agents to look at the content on the various sites, and think of how this type of content might work on their personal web sites. Remind agents to never copy material from someone else's site.

Step 7

Ask for any new thoughts or ideas before closing the meeting, and encourage each agent to come up with a different, catchy theme, and use the theme on everything! In all advertising, their web sites, promotional items, stationery, shirts, cars, and whatever else they do, promote, promote, promote their themes!

Finish the Sales Meeting With This Quote:

> *"In order to be irreplaceable one must always be different."* Gabrielle "Coco" Chanel (1883–1970) French designer of dresses, hats, sweaters, accessories, and perfume

ADDITIONAL NOTES TO COVER DURING MEEETING

Building Clients for Life

THEME: Building Clients for Life, Not Just for One Transaction!

ITEMS NEEDED:
- Flip chart
- Blank strips of paper
- Small trash can

ESTIMATED MEETING TIME:
- 10–15 minutes

MEETING OBJECTIVES:
- To explain the need to build clients for a lifetime and not just for a single transaction
- To allow agents to learn the importance of gathering good information about their clients and how to store and retrieve that data for future use. (*Note to the Broker/Manager:* Remind agents that information gathered about their clients is for their use and not to resell to outside vendors. Keeping clients' information private is important in today's information-gathering society)
- To help agents gain a better working knowledge of their former clients, what their clients' needs are, and how they can better serve them in the years to come. All of this will, in turn, lead to more repeat business and long-term trust and satisfaction between their agencies and clients.

MEETING APPLICATION:

Step 1

List the following statistics on the flip chart:

- The average length of time a seller has stayed in a home today is ____ years. *(Approximately five to seven years)*
- The average time a person keeps a home loan with a lender before paying it off is ____ years. *(Less than four years)*
- The average number of homes sold by an agent each year in our market area is ____.
- The percentage of people who used the same agent on their follow-up buy was ____.

Explain to the agents that building clients for a lifetime is important in our business.

Step 2

Ask the agents to write on a blank piece of paper the names of three to five clients they dealt with on a buying or selling transaction at least six months ago or longer.

Next, ask agents to estimate the number of times they have telephoned those clients since the closing and write that number next to their names. Stress that agents should list only the number that represents a "personal" phone call following up on how the clients were doing since the transaction.

Now, have the agents write next to the names the number of "personal" mailings that clients should have received from them. (*Note:* Encourage agents to not list weekly or monthly newsletters for this portion of the exercise. Stress the word "personal.")

Step 3

- Ask for agents who had to place a zero next to a client's name (stress that it's okay if they wrote zero for some) to raise their hands.
- Walk around with your small trash can and allow participants to place the papers with their clients' names with zeros into the empty basket.
- Mention that every time an agent fails to get back with a client, that client is being tossed into a large pool for other real estate agents to come along and snatch out.
- Have another agent reach into the trash can and pick a name out as you finish the last statement.
- This is also a good time to point out the following statistics from *The 2003 National Association of REALTORS® Profile of Home Buyers and Sellers.*
    - 74 percent of homebuyers said they would use the same real estate agent again.
    - 70 percent of sellers said they would use the same real estate agent again.

Ask the group:

- If the statistics are so great in homebuyers and sellers indicating they would use us again, why do we see our former clients so often use the services of our competitors?
- Are we staying in touch with our clients and customers like we should?
- How can we improve in this area? *Answer: good record-keeping, and staying in touch regularly with our past clients!*

Step 4

Explain that one way to draw repeat business is through good record-keeping after the sale, and gathering essential data before closing.

Separate the group into pairs and ask them to brainstorm and list the kinds of information that would be helpful to get from clients prior to or at the closing table. If your organization has a form it uses, go over the form with the group at this point.

Have everyone list suggestions of items that should be on the form and how the form could improve the company's long-term communication with clients.

Step 5

After several minutes ask the groups to share their lists with you, and write each point on the flip chart.

Begin with one side of the transaction, such as the seller, and cover the list that needs to go into a database and how a seller could use that information for future communication to the seller.

Do the same thing from the buyer's viewpoint.

If your company does not have an information gathering form for the agent to fill out at the closing table, take the list just developed with your agents and incorporate this into your closing practice. Develop a database in which to enter this information for easy retrieval in the future. Encourage agents to regularly follow up with their clients on a personal level in the future.

Step 6

Walk back around the room with the trash can and encourage agents to pull one or two strips of paper out. Explain that their clients don't even have to be in this pool of prospects for any real estate agent to snatch and take over.

Emphasize again one way to build clients for life: *"Stay in touch with them, and let them know you want their business for life, not just for a single transaction!"*

Finish the Sales Meeting With This Quote:

"It's easy to stop making mistakes. Just stop having ideas." Proverb

ADDITIONAL NOTES TO COVER DURING MEEETING

E-Newsletters (Part I)

(Note: You may also combine next week's meeting with this meeting if you prefer)

THEME: Creating E-Newsletters to Grab Your Customers' and Clients' Attention

ITEMS NEEDED:

- Timely article you can find on the Internet about home-ownership, tax tips, lawn care, or maintenance suggestions (Print out copies of these topics in advance.)
- A recent copy of your local newspaper
- Current issue of *TV Guide*®
- Copy of another national magazine
- Recent *Homes* magazine
- Recent piece of mail (regular U.S. postal mail) that you consider to be "junk mail," and would normally not open
- Recent e-mail that you did not ask for, sent to you in the attempt to market a product or service. (Keep in mind that it is important to use "junk mail" pieces both from the U.S. Postal Service and through your e-mail. Don't use marketing pieces that you openly subscribe to.)
- Flip chart
- Laptop computer and projector (optional)
  Note: If you do not have time to prepare for this meeting and cannot gather the necessary items needed, use a flip chart, and brainstorm with the group what types of articles would interest buyers and sellers. Ask also where you find these types of articles on the Internet.

ESTIMATED MEETING TIME:

- 15 minutes

continued...

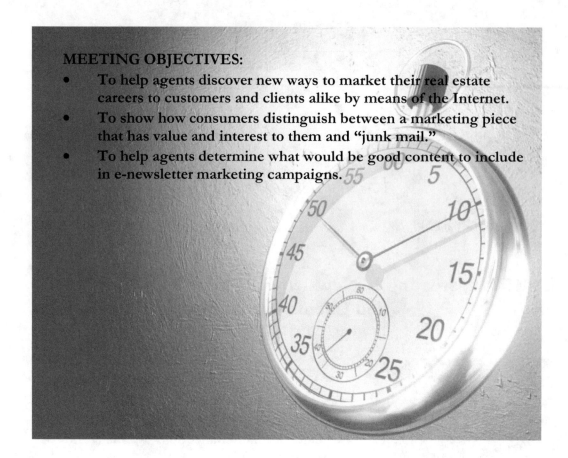

MEETING OBJECTIVES:

- To help agents discover new ways to market their real estate careers to customers and clients alike by means of the Internet.
- To show how consumers distinguish between a marketing piece that has value and interest to them and "junk mail."
- To help agents determine what would be good content to include in e-newsletter marketing campaigns.

MEETING APPLICATION:

Step 1

Begin by holding up the copy of your local newspaper and ask the group what is unique about this product.

Record answers on the flip chart if you like. Some suggestions should be that it contains news, it's local, it gets ink on my hands. Hopefully someone will mention that you have to pay for it, or it requires a subscription. If not, hold the thought for a moment.

Step 2

Repeat the same question for the *TV Guide* and national magazine you have chosen. Ask why someone would want to read these publications.

Again, you should record answers on the flip chart. Ask the following questions:

- Why would a person want to subscribe to the local paper versus the *TV Guide*?
- The national magazine?

Each publication contains information the person reading it would like to have. Naturally, the person reading the *TV Guide* has an interest in what's on the television channels and at what times. The national magazine has items of interest to its readers, and so on.

Step 3

Now hold up the local *Homes* guide and ask this question:

- What does this product have that the consumer wants more information about?

Answers should include information about homes; which ones are for sale; finding an agent; and other related issues. Now ask:

- What's different between the *Homes* magazine and the other publications?

Besides content, you should hear someone say that one is free and the others are not.

Step 4

Finally, hold up the two pieces of junk mail, one received at home through the U.S. Mail and the other through your e-mail program. Point out that, in your eyes, both unsolicited marketing pieces are "junk mail." Both were on their way to the trash can, and you had no use or purpose for the information mailed to you.

Explain that one distinction between the various publications and marketing pieces lies in the fact that some of these pieces are "opt-in" and others are "opt-out." In other words, if I buy a *TV Guide* at the grocery store, I have in essence "opted-in" for that publication. On the other hand, the mass e-mail sent to me is in an area where I want to "opt-out;" frankly, I never agreed to receive their mailing. Normally, most people who receive these types of marketing tactics make one response on their computers: DELETE.

Our goal in developing a good e-mail newsletter distribution list is to encourage people (clients, customers, friends, and others) to "opt-in." In other words, we want them to sign-up for our newsletter, which leads us to our next question, how do we do that? How do we get people to "opt-in" to receive our mailings?

The answer is that we first build good content to include in our newsletter, and second, we ask them to sign up.

Step 5

Begin with building content. Use the following questions to stimulate interest among your members:

- Why do consumers buy *TV Guide*? *To get information about what is playing on TV*
- Overall, why do people buy the local newspaper? *To get local news*
- Why do people buy the magazine you are displaying? *It provides some item of interest for them.*
- Why do people pick up the *Homes* guide? *To receive information on the homes market, as they could have an immediate or future interest in buying or selling a home.*
- What are the top five concerns of a person buying a home?
- What are the top five concerns of a person selling a home?

- What do most sellers want to know about other homes that have recently sold in their subdivisions?
- What are most homebuyers looking for before finding a home to buy?

You should by now have a good basis of what it is most people are looking for when they buy or sell a home. Tie in the fact that our goal should be to make people want to subscribe to our service (e-newsletter), and to do this we must offer information the consumer feels is of interest to him or her.

Step 6

Explain that next week's meeting is on getting people to "opt-in" for your e-newsletter. (*Note:* You may also combine next week's meeting with this meeting if you prefer). As a homework assignment, have agents think of ideas that consumers might find interesting and might prompt them to sign up for your monthly newsletter. Also, brainstorm other possible topics to include each month throughout the year. Give a prize for the group or agents who can come up with the most ideas. (If you choose to use this meeting in combination with the next e-newsletter meeting, be sure to ask for the homework assignments in advance of the meeting).

Encourage agents to develop templates that they can use each month for their newsletters. If an agent already has an e-newsletter in place, encourage him or her to bring a sample to share with the group. It is also an excellent idea to have your group research companies through the Internet to find sample e-newsletter templates and costs. (*Hint:* If the agents visit a web site such as http://www.google.com and type in e-newsletter templates, they should get several choices.)

Finish the Sales Meeting With This Quote:

> *"The two words 'information' and 'communication' are often used interchangeably, but they signify quite different things. Information is giving out; communication is getting through."*
> Sydney J. Harris (1917–1986) American journalist, author.

ADDITIONAL NOTES TO COVER DURING MEEETING

E-Newsletters (Part II)

THEME: Insuring that E-Mail Marketing Is Always Done On an "Opt-In" Basis

ITEMS NEEDED:

- Flip chart
- Homework assignments given out from previous meeting

ESTIMATED MEETING TIME:

- 10–15 minutes

MEETING OBJECTIVE:

- To stress to agents the need to have consumers and clients "opt-in" or subscribe to their e-newsletters and not to send unsolicited e-mail
- To develop a list of ideas that will make consumers want to sign up for monthly e-newsletters
- To explore options for allowing consumers to sign up for e-newsletters automatically

MEETING APPLICATION:

Step 1

On a new sheet of paper on your flip chart, ask for volunteers to share their answers from the homework assignment. If you have a prize or prizes for the most creative or the greatest number of ideas, don't forget to hand out the awards. Following is a list of items to be covered in the homework assignments.

- Ideas for your newsletter
- Ways to get consumers to sign up for your newsletter
- E-newsletter template ideas and or companies who provide a product like this

Step 2

Before the meeting, write the various months of the year as shown below on your flip chart. Record the answers on your flip chart and discuss them with the group

Ask the group this question:

- What is some information that you could include each month in your newsletter?

Some possible suggestions you can share are listed below:

- January–March: Offer tax tips, Christmas Club ideas for the following year, gardening tips, and good chili or soup recipes.
- April–May: Gardening ideas are still good. Also appropriate would be lawn care tips, spring-cleaning hints, tips on tax planning for the next year, summer camp suggestions for children, and salad recipes.
- June–August: Offer vacation tips and lawn suggestions.
- September–October: This is a good time for insulation ideas and energy tips, and pumpkin and fall decorative ideas and recipes.
- November–December: Suggest family get-together ideas, guides for holiday planning, and seasonal recipes.

Step 3

Ask the group this question:

- What are some ideas or ways to draw consumers to your company or agent web site?

List the responses on the flip chart. Listed below are some ideas that might come up during the discussion.

- Send out a letter to people within your sphere of influence and/or area and ask them if they would like to receive this e-newsletter. Note that Greg Hobbs and Tom Herder (from the marketing firm of Hobbs and Herder) suggest that you should do this four times over a 45-day period to the same group of people. Use the same letter, but be sure to send it out four times. By doing this you should get a 20 percent response rate for subscribers to your letter

- Place information about your e-newsletter in all of your mailings and promotional pieces. Example copy might say: *Be the first to know about great buys in Oak Woods Terrace! Subscribe to my monthly e-newsletter today! Call or send me your e-mail address.* Or, *Would you like to know what homes are selling for in your neighborhood? I provide an average sales price and days on market for the following communities in my monthly newsletter. Subscribe today by calling or sending me your e-mail address.*
- Place a spot on your web site where visitors can subscribe online.
- Volunteer to send out information for the local soccer or baseball league to the parents on practices and game times.
- Volunteer for your place of worship or civic organization to e-mail monthly reminders about upcoming events.
- Offer to send out listings of new books the local library has received for those wishing to subscribe to a list.

Explain to the group that the key is to put yourself in a position to provide a value service to others. If, in the process, one or two people subscribe to your newsletter, that's an added benefit.

Step 4

The final area the group researched in advance was with e-newsletter templates. Discuss ideas and samples generated with the group. If no one brings a sample newsletter to use, have the groups take a few minutes to develop a sample newsletter by sketching what would look good.

Step 5

Ask the group these additional questions:

- How often should you put out a newsletter?
- Is an e-newsletter something you want to do?
- Should you develop your own e-newsletter or subscribe to a generic newsletter already constructed for you?
- How will you (or do you) distribute your e-newsletter?
- What are some items you should always include with your e-newsletter? *Free price evaluation, properties for sale, ways to get in touch with you by phone or via the Internet*

Step 6

Encourage the group to consider setting up monthly e-newsletters, if they have not done so. Stress the benefits of utilizing this marketing method to save time and money and at the same time reach hundreds of consumers in a matter of seconds.

Remind the agents that, like any method of prospecting, the key is doing it on a regular basis and always asking for the business!

Finish the Sales Meeting With This Quote:

"Creativity is so delicate a flower that praise tends to make it bloom, while discouragement often nips it in the bud." Unknown

<u>ADDITIONAL NOTES TO COVER DURING MEEETING</u>

MARKETING MEETING

6

MLS® Signatures

THEME: Using Signatures on Your Desktop Can Save You a Lot of Time and Typing

ITEMS NEEDED:
- Laptop computer
- Overhead projector
  If you cannot provide a computer and projector, you could still print out hard copies from the CD to give out to the group.

A word of caution for this sales meeting: if you are not skillful with computers or technology, ask someone from your office who is more knowledgeable to read over this meeting idea and deliver it for you. Not all Multiple Listing Services (MLS®) work in the same manner; so you may need to make some changes to make this meeting fit your needs.

ESTIMATED MEETING TIME:
- 10–15 minutes

MEETING OBJECTIVE:
- To help agents develop a standard set of prewritten e-mail messages that they use often, to save them valuable time and energy in responding to customer and client inquires through their daily e-mail

MEETING APPLICATION:

Step 1

The type of MLS® your organization subscribes to (if you are a member of a local MLS®) and the type of inquiries you receive weekly will dictate the direction of this meeting. Even when buyers visit our personal web sites, most ask the same question: *"Can you give me more information on this property?"* If this does not describe your present business scenario, prepare yourself, because the Internet is fast becoming the new way of shopping for most homebuyers.

Explain that according to the *National Association of REALTORS® Profile of Home Buyers and Sellers*, 2003, 65 percent of buyers used the Internet to search for a home. This is the first year that the Internet has surpassed newspaper advertisement as a means for home searches by consumers. Those are amazing statistics that will only continue to rise in the future. As more and more consumers use e-mail as a basis of communication for their first contact about information on property, you must be ready to respond in a fast and timely manner.

Explain to agents that this meeting will show them how to "save" more time with prewritten e-mails, or what others might refer to as "signatures," for use with their e-mail programs.

Step 2

Ask the agents the following questions:

- Do you currently receive e-mails from customers or clients that ask the same questions over and again? For example, in the last two or three months, has more than one party requested more information on a property?
- Did you write different messages to those clients?
- What are some other types of e-mails that you send out regularly that contain the same information, but you re-type each time you send?

Explain to the agents that one way to save a lot of time and energy is to create a folder on the desktop of your computer that holds prewritten e-mail messages inside for later retrieval.

Step 3

Discuss this example:

- Suppose you receive an e-mail from someone who wants to know more information about listing number 9502424. Normally you would look this listing up in the MLS® or your company web site and database and send an e-mail back with the information requested. That response might be through an attached document that contains all the information or, like most communications sent by MLS® vendors today, it would probably contain a "link." The web address link lets the person on the other end click on it and go right to the web site with the property information. Whatever method you use, you still need to add some personal dialogue with your e-mail. This is where our prewritten e-mail message (or signature) will come into play. Hand out the following prewritten e-mail message (contained on resources CD):

Dear M_ _____ :

Thank you so much for the e-mail. I have attached a link below for you to preview this listing. If you would like more information or would like to arrange an appointment to preview this home please give me a call.

Would you like to be the first to hear about new listings that might interest you? If so, reply to this message and give me a brief description about what you are looking for. I can set up a special search for you in our MLS® so any new listings will go directly to your e-mail. Please keep in mind that some of the listings might be with another real estate firm; however, you can still put my 25 years of real estate experience to work for you. Just call me and I can take care of all the needed details.

Again, thanks for the e-mail, and I hope to hear from you soon.

John Mayfield, ePRO, ABR®, ABRM^SM, GRI
Broker, Owner - Mayfield GMAC Real Estate
Farmington, MO Ph: 573.756.0077 Fax: 573.756.1336
Web Site: http://www.MayfieldRE.com

Point out that the e-mail message is generic and formatted for anyone inquiring about a piece of property. All the agent has to do is add the greeting line (e.g., Dear Mr. & Mrs. Smith) and the e-mail message is ready to send. Sounds simple enough, but explain to the agents there are also a couple of other issues that need to be resolved.

Step 4

What if the inquiry asked about more than one property? What if the e-mail asked about commercial listings or a farm? The answer is simple: design your e-mails so that whatever the inquiry, the message fits the subject matter. This way, each response looks tailored for the type of inquiry. For example, use the following e-mail when someone asks about land listings:

Dear M_. _____ :

Thank you so much for the e-mail. I have attached a link below for you to view the various land listings you requested. If you would like more information or plats for any of these listings please let me know.

Would you like to be the first to hear about new land listings? If so, reply to this message and give me a brief description to what you are looking for. I can set up a special search for you in our MLS® so any new land listings will go directly to your e-mail. Please keep in mind that some of the listings might be with another real estate firm; however, you can still put my 25 years of real estate experience to work for you.

Again thanks for the e-mail!

John Mayfield, ePRO, ABR®, ABRM^SM , GRI
Broker Owner - Mayfield GMAC Real Estate
Farmington, MO Ph: 573.756.0077 Fax: 573.756.1336
Web Site: http://www.mayfieldhomes.com

Tell the agents that this e-mail works for inquiries received about land listings in their marketplaces. Tell them to be as creative as they like: if they work primarily in a particular subdivision and their e-mails are for this subdivision, have the e-mail incorporate those words to add a personal touch. Remind the group that saving time is essential in the real estate business, and organizing repeated types of e-mails will be a lifesaver during busy and hectic days.

Step 5

If time allows and you would like the group to brainstorm some additional prewritten letters to use, allow them the opportunity to get into groups and develop letters to share with the entire office. There are additional sample letters on the resource CD you may copy and distribute to the group if you choose, and a handout for explaining to agents how to copy and paste text from one software program to another.

Finish the Sales Meeting With This Quote:

"Why kill time when one can employ it?" French proverb

<u>ADDITIONAL NOTES TO COVER DURING MEEETING</u>

MARKETING
MEETING

7

Preparing Your Case

THEME: Presenting Your Case

ITEMS NEEDED:
- Flip chart
- Handout from resource CD

ESTIMATED MEETING TIME:
- 10–15 minutes

MEETING OBJECTIVES:
- To remind agents of the importance of building a case for why buyers and sellers should accept an offer or counteroffer
- To encourage agents to use a plan of action when preparing to present offers and counteroffers to buyers, sellers, and agents
- To point out to everyone that preparation is key when presenting offers and counteroffers to all parties in a real estate transaction

MEETING APPLICATION:

Step 1

Have agents get into groups of two or three and read the following stories from the CD. Take one story at a time and discuss the points of interest with the group.

Story 1:

Bob and Brenda Smith list their house at 1651 Rector Lane, Newberry, Missouri, with you. Bob and Brenda owe $175,000 on a first deed of trust, and $35,000 on a second deed of trust. You prepare a CMA on the Smiths' home and the suggested list price is $225,000. Your office charges 7 percent commission. The estimated closing costs for this sale are $1,500. The Smiths point out to you that they do not want to pay a buyer's agent a fee and will pay only 6 percent to your firm if you sell it. Bob and Brenda need to sell their home since Bob lost his job. The average time on market for the Smiths' subdivision is 75 days, at an average sales price of $218,500. The Smiths will sign a 90-day listing agreement on an exclusive agency agreement. You agree to the listing terms with the Smiths, and place a for-sale sign in the front yard.

The following week John Davis from XYZ Realty inquires about the Smiths' listing and asks if he can show the property later that same day. John suggests to you that he will be working as a buyer's agent, and his client will pay him a fee for his services.

Later that night John calls you with an offer to buy on the Smiths' home. The offer is for $215,000 cash. John needs an answer that same night as his buyers are leaving the next day and would like to offer on another home if the Smiths will not accept this offer.

Answer the following questions:

- If the Smiths accepted this offer to purchase, what would their estimated net proceeds be?
- Would you recommend that Bob and Brenda accept this offer?
- If not, what would your suggested response to John be? In other words, how would you present your counteroffer to John?
- If the Smiths asked you why they should take this offer, what reasons would you list for them?
- What additional information would help you in your recommendation to the Smiths?

Story 2:

You visit the home of Ron and Jessica Neighbors at 331 Meadowbrook Drive. The Neighbors would like to sell their two-story home in the Weatherwood Subdivision. After gathering the necessary information on the Neighbors' home, you go back to your office and prepare a comparative market analysis (CMA). In your research you determine the Neighbors home is worth around $235,000 to $240,000. You also discover the average sales price in Weatherwood falls into this same price bracket. The number of days on market for Weatherwood homes is 92. The demand for one-story homes is stronger than that for two-story, and the most expensive home for sale in Weatherwood is $248,500.

After you present your CMA to the Neighbors, they say to you that they would like to net $240,000 for their home. You discover that they owe around $217,000, but refinanced their home to pay off a credit card debt of $30,000. In the Neighbors' mind they think they have over $235,000 in their home, since this is what they refinanced their loan for several years ago. The Neighbors explain to you that Johnson Realty looked at their home and will list it for $259,900.

Based on the information provided to you, answer the following questions:
- How will you explain to the Neighbors that $259,900 is too much for their house?
- Would you take the listing?
- Why or why not?
- If you agree to take the listing, what measures would you put into place to assure that the property might sell?
- What would be your response to the Neighbors about Johnson Realty agreeing to the higher list price?

Story 3:
Traveling around Briargate Subdivision you notice a for-sale-by-owner sign (FSBO) and call the number on the sign. After a conversation with the owner you set up an appointment to preview the home later that day. Your visit goes very well, and you feel like you have a good rapport with the homeowners; however, during the visit they stress to you that they do not want to list with a real estate company. They have had many people come through and look at their home, and they even sold their last home by themselves.

Answer the following questions:

- What would be your response to the sellers before you leave their home?
- Would you try to list their property at this point?
- Why or why not?
- How could you get a second visit with the FSBOs?

Have your group develop a thirty-day marketing plan to stay in touch with these prospects without being too pushy.

Story 4:
Larry and Jane Eversole's listing with you is about to expire. You have had their home listed for three months. During this 90-day listing you have had many lookers at their home, but no offers. You have always felt the price they are asking for their home to be too high. The Eversoles' home is in a great location, and you feel their home could sell if they would adjust the price by fifteen or twenty thousand dollars. You plan to visit the Eversoles this evening with your extension agreement and a price reduction form, and fear that they may list their property with another agency.
Based on the information, answer the following questions:

- Would you continue the Eversoles' listing?
- Why or why not?
- What would your approach be to convince the Eversoles to reduce their list price?

- What supporting material or documents would you take with you to your appointment this evening?
- The Eversoles say that people can always make an offer if they think the price is too high, and ask you why no one has done that. What will be your response?
- The Eversoles wonder if taking it off market during the winter months would be better, and to wait until spring to try to sell. What would be your response?

If you have additional case studies you have faced in your marketplace, feel free to write out sample scenarios to include in your meeting.

Step 2

Remind the agents that the purpose of this meeting is to demonstrate the need for preparation when we work with buyers or sellers. Encourage the group to think about possible situations they have faced in the past, and to prepare sample presentations that they can reconstruct quickly to use in their business.

Finish the Sales Meeting With This Quote:

"One important key to success is self-confidence. An important key to self-confidence is preparation." Arthur Ashe (1943–1993) American college & pro tennis champion, first black international tennis champion.

ADDITIONAL NOTES TO COVER DURING MEEETING

MARKETING
MEETING

8

Direct Mail

THEME: Utilizing Direct Mail Properly to Make it Fun, Profitable, and Well Worth the Time

ITEMS NEEDED:

- Flip chart
- Laptop computer (optional)
- Overhead projector
- PowerPoint slide show from Resource CD
- Two handouts from the resource CD

ESTIMATED MEETING TIME:

- 15 minutes

MEETING OBJECTIVES:

- To encourage agents to use direct mail marketing with their prospecting measures
- To show agents the need to be creative and different when utilizing the direct mail method for prospecting
- To help agents develop a list of direct mail ideas to use in their day-to-day prospecting methods

MEETING APPLICATION:

Step 1

Ask the group the following questions, and record their responses on the flip chart:

- Is direct mail a good idea for real estate agents?
- Why or why not?
- If you were planning on implementing a direct mail program, what are some things you would need to consider?
- What should your direct mail piece contain?

 Provide the following fact sheet for your agents as quoted by the Ambrose Printing Company's web site found on the resource CD:

1. There are approximately 12 billion pieces of bulk mail sent each year in the United States.
2. For every dollar spent on bulk mail, the average return on investment is $10.00.
3. If you use direct mailing on a consistent basis, you can normally expect to increase your business by approximately 7 percent.
4. Bulk mail accounts for approximately 50 percent of the mail handled by the U.S. Postal service.
5. A direct mail piece offering an incentive will generally increase your response rate by four times more than a marketing piece without an incentive.
6. Approximately 50 percent of bulk mail is opened and read.
7. Of the 50 percent who open and read bulk mail, 40 percent found the information useful.
8. The first postmaster of the United States was Benjamin Franklin. He used direct mail to raise funds for a local hospital and to offer replacement parts and accessories for his Franklin stoves.
9. Promotional material that offers a bind-in tear-out that a consumer can reply to increases the response rate by 600 percent more than those pieces without a pull-out.
10. Generally, only 10 percent to 20 percent of the success of a direct mail program can be attributed to the creativeness of the marketing piece. Most of the success of a direct mailing is due to the list of recipients and the type of promotional item being offered.

Step 2

After you have reviewed the direct mail facts, ask the group the following question:

- After reading the information on the handout, what do you think your direct mail campaign should focus on?

<u>Direct Mail Idea</u>

This is an idea that I got from a good friend of mine, Corky Hyatt, who is an instructor and trainer in Kansas.

Ask your agents to close their eyes, pretend to go to the mailbox, and describe in detail the pieces of mail there. After the agents have closed their eyes, read the following to them:

You are walking out to get your mail. Visualize where your mailbox is located. It's a warm, sunny day and you just finished listing a beautiful home that is priced to sell. You have a closing later in the day and you stopped by your home to eat a quick bite of lunch and check your mail. After gathering the large bundle of mail you begin to sift through the pieces one by one. The utility bill is enclosed, along with the monthly phone bill. You notice a couple of credit card offers, a circular to the local department store, and a large brown envelope that is pushing magazine subscriptions. There's your car payment bill. You begin to wonder how these bills can come around so quickly each month. Did you remember to tell the buyers to have their cashier's check made out to the escrow agent? Your mind continues to wander as you head for the house. You notice on the bottom of the stack of mail that you just retrieved an odd-shaped envelope that has been hand-addressed to you. The penmanship looks very impressive and there is only a street name and number in the return address portion of the envelope.

Ask the group which piece of mail will they open first.

An overwhelming majority will probably be in favor of opening the off-size envelope that has been personally addressed. Why? Because it's different, and it is "personalized!"

Step 3

Another good idea to stress to the group is the use of a handwritten font when mail merging through a word processing program. The consumer will perceive a handwritten font as being more personal and interesting, increasing the odds of the marketing piece being opened. Use different-size envelopes. Card shops sometimes have extra envelopes that they may sell you at a reduced price. Odd-sized envelopes will also help to make your piece stand out and get opened. Try to avoid sending your direct mail between the first and the fifteenth of the month Many billing statements are sent at this time and you might get lost in the shuffle.

 Which marketing piece would get more attention (available on resource CD to distribute to the group)?

Sample 1:
(Garamond Font)

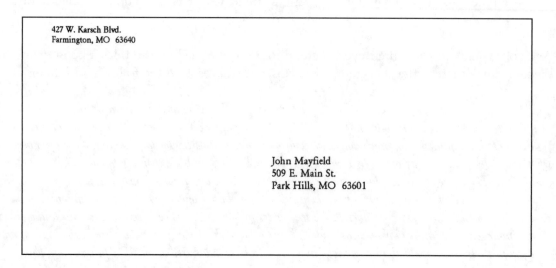

or

Sample 2:
(Bradley Hand Font)

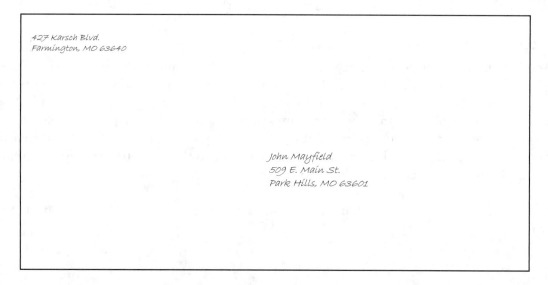

The handwritten font will probably receive more attention and be more intriguing to the recipient than the standard font with which so many documents are addressed.

Remind the agents that if they do not have a handwritten font already installed on their computers, they can normally find a selection on the Internet as a "free" download.

Step 4

Don't forget to *keep it ethical*. Be careful to not solicit homeowners who currently have their property under contract with another agency. Check your state laws prior to performing any type of mass mail program. However, you may do a mass mailing and not have to verify everyone on the list to stay in compliance with the National Association of REALTORS® code of ethics Article 16 and Standard of Practice 16-2.

Have agents break into small groups and develop a list of direct mail marketing ideas that they could use in prospecting for new business.

Examples should include:
- *Just Listed* Postcards
- *Just Sold* Postcards
- General information postcards
- Tax advice
- Financial help
- Mortgage rates
- Subdivision sales prices
- Average sold price, days on market, new listings, etc.

Write the responses on the flip chart. Encourage agents to be creative and set goals to implement some of the suggested ideas that they feel comfortable with. Remind agents that one of the highest factors for considering the use of direct mail is the promotional item being offered. Always offer "something" in your direct marketing piece! A "FREE" price evaluation is an excellent example of a service they can offer. Before offering gifts of value as consideration, make sure you check with your state's real estate law to see what is and is not prohibited.

Step 5

Have agents look at the handout you provided them at the beginning of the meeting from the Ambrose Printing Company web site. Ask the agents to read the third fact on the sheet.

- If you use direct mailing on a consistent basis, you can normally expect to increase your business by approximately 7 percent.

Now have the agents read the fifth fact again.

- A direct mail piece offering an incentive will generally increase your response rate by four times more than a marketing piece without an incentive.

Repeat the same process for facts six and seven.

- Approximately 50 percent of bulk mail is opened and read.
- Of the 50 percent who open and read bulk mail, 40 percent found the information useful.

Remind the group that if they use direct mail on a consistent basis, and follow the guidelines of others, direct mail can be fun, profitable, and well worth the time spent!

Finish the Sales Meeting With This Quote:

> *"Nothing echoes like an empty mailbox."* Charles M. Schulz, Creator of *Peanuts*, United Feature Syndicate

ADDITIONAL NOTES TO COVER DURING MEEETING

Working with First-Time Buyers

THEME: Helping Agents Understand the Questions and Issues Most First-Time Homebuyers Face When Purchasing a Home

ITEMS NEEDED:

- Flip chart
- Detailed instructions on putting together a computer desk, bicycle, or other complicated object
- Advance copies of the instructions for each agent, or, if you prefer to conserve paper, you can have agents get into small groups, and give one set to each group
  Note: A PowerPoint slide show has been included on the resource CD if you have a computer and projector to use during your meeting

ESTIMATED MEETING TIME:

- 15 minutes

MEETING OBJECTIVES:

- To help agents understand the questions and issues most first-time homebuyers face when purchasing a home
- To help agents learn the latest statistics for first-time homebuyers
- To encourage agents to examine the characteristics of the first-time homebuyer
- To allow agents to brainstorm ideas for information that could be included in a presentation tailored specifically for the first-time homebuyer

MEETING APPLICATION:

Step 1

Pass out the detailed instructions if you chose to have this visual with your meeting. Hopefully the list of steps for putting together this product will help illustrate your point as to how complicated something is to someone who has absolutely no knowledge as to what is going on. If you prefer, copy a sample mortgage or deed of trust or other legal document that may look complicated or difficult to understand.

Step 2

Pass out a blank piece of paper and have agents write in the correct responses that go with each acronym:

- LTV   *Loan-to-Value Ratio*
- PITI   *Principal, Interest, Taxes and Insurance*
- MIP   *Mortgage Interest Premium*
- Title Insurance   *Insurance that will guarantee there are no liens or certain kinds of encumbrances against the property. Indicates the current owners have the right to transfer title to the property, along with several other guarantees for the purchaser of title insurance*
- GRI   *Graduate REALTOR® Institute*
- CRS   *Certified Residential Specialist*
- ABR   *Accredited Buyer's Representative*
- Mortgage Survey   *A survey that "does not" actually set any corners, but examines the property and reports on whether there are any encroachments or not*
- Comparable Property   *A property that is used in an appraisal that is similar in physical condition, time of the sale, and in a close proximity to the subject property that is under evaluation*
- Subject Property   *The property that is being appraised*
- Debt to Equity Ratio   *Ratios that are used by lenders to determine if the borrower is qualified to make the required monthly mortgage payment on their proposed loan*

Step 3

Now have agents complete the following medical acronyms as you read the initials. You may also use the PowerPoint slide show for this portion of the exercise.

- CJD   *Creutzfeldt-Jakob Disease*
- CCP   *Chronic Calcifying Pancreatitis*
- DFR   *Dialysate Filtration Rate*
- LIV   *Left Innominate Vein*

Hopefully, after a few medical acronyms, the agents will get the picture that, for many first-time homebuyers, our vocabulary makes no sense to them. Ask agents for other words that are used in our industry that first-time homebuyers (or homebuyers in general) may not understand.

Step 4

Next, have agents rank the following items 1–11, in the order that they will take place during a typical home purchase (with "1" being the first item to be completed after a sales contract has been accepted, and "11" the last item to be completed).

_____ Appraisal
_____ Loan application
_____ Contract
_____ Order title insurance
_____ Inspections
_____ Obtaining homeowners insurance
_____ Closing
_____ Possession of new home
_____ Loan approval
_____ Order survey
_____ Final walk-through

Step 5

Ask the group the following questions:

- Where is a good point for an agent to begin when working with a first-time homebuyer?
- How big is the first-time homebuyer market in the United States? *Answer: According to the 2003 NAR* (NATIONAL ASSOCIATION OF REALTORS®) Profile of Home Buyers and Sellers, *40 percent of all homebuyers in the survey were first-time homebuyers.*

> Other statistics for first-time homebuyers from the *2003 NAR Profile of Home Buyers and Sellers* (NATIONAL ASSOCIATION OF REALTORS®):
> - Generally younger in age than the typical homebuyer
> - Income levels are less than repeat homebuyers
> - Average age in 2003 for a first-time homebuyer was 32 years old. This is about fourteen years younger than the average age of repeat buyers
> - Average income for a first-time homebuyer, according to the NAR report, showed a figure of $54,800, which is $19,800 lower than that of repeat homebuyers
> - First-time homebuyers play a large role for real estate agents and, according to the NAR report, they account for two-fifths of all homebuyers during the last ten years

Step 6

Have agents get into groups and develop a list of possible information they could put into a presentation to use with first-time homebuyers. After the groups have had enough time to come up with a sample story-board presentation, ask for volunteers to share their results with the group.

Finish the Sales Meeting With This Quote:

> *"There's a great power in words, if you don't hitch too many of them together."* Josh Billings, pseudonym of Henry Wheeler Shaw (1856–1950) Irish playwright & critic

ADDITIONAL NOTES TO COVER DURING MEEETING

Working with Senior Adults

THEME: Working with the Senior Adult Population Can Be a Rewarding Experience

ITEMS NEEDED:
- Flip chart
- Projector (optional)
- Photo album
- Small child's book
- An item of sentiment that was left to you by a parent or grandparent whom you cherished
- PowerPoint show on resource CD

ESTIMATED MEETING TIME:
- 15–20 minutes

MEETING OBJECTIVES:
- To explore the various issues senior adults are faced with when buying and selling a home
- To develop a listing and buyers' presentation that is geared specifically to the senior adult population

MEETING APPLICATION:

Step 1

Begin the meeting by presenting the following facts and figures:

- According to the Seniors Real Estate Specialists, (SRES) web site, 11 states (Nevada [70 percent growth], followed by Alaska [25%], Arizona, New Mexico, Hawaii, Utah, and Colorado) experienced faster growth with the senior adult population than Florida.
- Other states that experienced growth of 19 percent or more were South Carolina, Texas, North Carolina and Georgia.
- Another vital statistic is that, according to the U.S. Census statistics, approximately 13 percent of our population is now over the age of 65. That equates to one in eight.
- Couple this with a longer life expectancy (the average is now 85 for women and 76 for men), and agents will realize that the senior market is **big** and getting bigger each day.
- Understanding and knowing how to market to this segment is the focus of today's sales meeting idea.

Step 2

Have participants complete the following questions and assignments:

- What is the first book you remember reading as a child?
- Do you remember what you liked about that book as a child?
- List one item in your home that is of value you to you, and not necessarily because of its worth.
- Why did you list the item in the previous question?
- List one thing you did in your home as a child that you look back on and laugh about now.
- How many times did you move during your school years?
- How many times have your parents moved during your life?
    - a. 1–5
    - b. 5–10
    - c. 10+

Step 3

Have the agents write down whether the following statements are *True* or *False*:

- The senior population is one of the fastest growing segments of our country's population. _____
- Most seniors have the same needs. _____
- Most seniors are worried more about running out of money before they die. _____

After the agents have had time to complete the quiz, talk about the items you have displayed in front, along with the responses and answers from the quiz. Answers are *True, False, True.*

Step 4

Write the following on your flip chart:

Family photo album	=	Memories
Children's book	=	Simple and easy to understand
Favorite item	=	Undeterminable value and feelings

Elaborate on the photo album and explain that, as with any photo album, there are "memories" involved.

Talk about the personal item left to you by a parent or grandparent. This will show the priceless nature of many items in our homes and the deep-rooted feelings attached to them.

Finally, the children's book is an excellent illustration to show how books that seemed detailed and important to us as children look basic and simplistic today. Point out that for you and me as real estate agents the transaction might seem generic and easy to understand; however for the senior many things may have changed in the real estate transaction process since his or her last purchase or sale.

Step 5

According to the Seniors Real Estate Specialists (SRES) web site, most seniors live in the same home for approximately 26.8 years, unlike our current first-time homebuyer who moves every five to seven years.

Write the word **TIME** on your flip chart.

Ask agents if they can guess what the word *time* has to do with working with seniors.

- Most seniors do not like to rush into the decision making process.

Tell your agents to always allow seniors enough time to think through and weigh all alternatives before closing the deal. One excellent way agents can accomplish this is to have a detailed and tailored marketing campaign directly aimed at seniors.

Finally, remind agents that working with seniors will require patience. One of the principles learned in earning the SRES designation is how to use the skill of patience.

As mentioned above, a delicate and different type of marketing technique will need to be implemented for dealing with seniors. They have different concerns from most homebuyers and sellers. Encourage agents to read articles and/or search the web at for additional information about seniors and the real estate industry.

Step 6

Ask the following questions and write the responses on the flip chart:

- What are some various issues you have faced while working with senior adults?
- How can we develop a marketing plan to work with seniors, and what would be some good information to include in our plan?
- If you developed a presentation booklet or flyer for senior adults, what would you want to include?
- What would be a good seminar to hold geared solely toward the senior adult market?
- What is the senior adult population for our area? (You can normally get this in advance at http://www.census.gov
- Do you have any other ideas on working with seniors?

Finish the Sales Meeting With This Quote:

"We neither get better or worse as we get older, but more like ourselves."
Dr. Robert Anthony (1916–) American management educator, author, U.S. Assistant Secretary of Defense. *Think, Think On and Think Again.*

<u>ADDITIONAL NOTES TO COVER DURING MEEETING</u>

Prospecting
Meetings

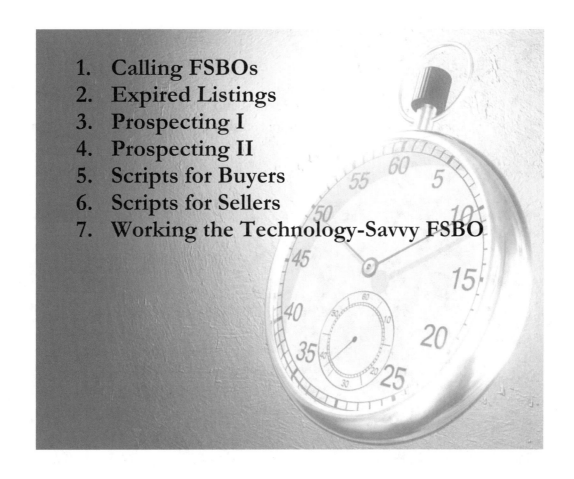

Calling FSBOs

THEME: Calling the For-Sale-By-Owner (FSBO) Can Be a Profitable and Rewarding Experience

ITEMS NEEDED:
- Flip chart
- Newspaper with real estate ad section
- Sample sales contract you currently use and all forms, disclosures, and addenda

ESTIMATED MEETING TIME:
- 15 minutes

MEETING OBJECTIVES:
- To show agents a new plan for calling the for-sale-by-owner (FSBO)
- To show agents how to carry out this plan on a weekly basis to increase their listing base and market share for new listings
- To talk about any no-call lists applicable to you on a state or federal level, and to point out that calls should be generated only when the consumer invites the phone call

MEETING APPLICATION:

Step 1
Hold up the forms needed for the average sales contract in your office, and remind your agents that this is the paperwork needed for the average sales contract. You might even mention the number of pages included in the set of papers you are holding in your hand.

Step 2
Next, write the word **PAPERWORK** on your flip chart. Explain to the group that understanding and completing the paperwork involved in a real estate transaction is the number-one concern for FSBOs in the selling process, according to *The 2003 National Association of REALTORS® Profile of Home Buyers and Sellers.*

Step 3
Write the words **Other** and **Price** respectively under *PAPERWORK*, and tell the group that these are the two additional big concerns to FSBOs. (Of FSBO concerns, 20 percent rated *paperwork* highest, and 15 percent rated *other* highest. Setting the right price was a concern of only 9 percent of the FSBOs.)

Advise those in the group who already have a plan that works for calling the FSBO, to use it, and encourage them to share some of their tips with the others following the presentation.

Step 4
Ask the group the following questions, and write their responses on your flip chart. (*Note:* The answers to each question are from *The 2003 National Association of REALTORS® Profile of Home Buyers and Sellers.*)

- Why do most FSBOs want to sell on their own? *The answer given most will probably be to save the commission. 46 percent answered this as their highest reason to sell on their own.*
- Do you think most FSBOs understand the process? *As mentioned earlier, 30 percent of FSBOs had difficulty completing the paperwork.*
- Do you think most FSBOs are in a hurry to sell? *55 percent were no hurry to sell their homes, compared with only 42 percent of sellers who had real estate agents help them. (Note: This statistic was taken from the same study noted above, but for the year 2002.)*
- Do you think most FSBOs will allow real estate agents to preview their homes? *In general most FSBOs will be open for real estate agents to preview their homes.*
- Do you think most FSBOs use their friends, family, and neighbors as a big source to sell their homes? *27 percent of the respondents to the survey listed this as their fourth highest means to aid them in selling their homes. 72 percent said a yard signs were their primary avenues for marketing their homes, and 61 percent used the newspaper.*
- Do you think FSBO homes sold for more or less than real-estate-agent-assisted homes, according to The 2003 National Association of REALTORS® Profile of Home Buyers and Sellers? *The median sales price for an FSBO was $145,000 while the agent-assisted home sold for an average of $175,000.*
- How do you think successful FSBOs will react the next time they need to sell their homes? Will they use agents or sell their homes themselves? *50 percent of the respondents*

to The 2003 National Association of REALTORS® Profile of Home Buyers and Sellers *pointed out that they would sell their houses themselves if they had to do it over again. 13 percent would hire real estate agents the next time, and 37 percent were not sure what they would do.*

Step 5

Explain that the process you are about to use has been successful in calling on FSBOs, and it should contain some new insights for calling the FSBO.

Ask for a volunteer to read the first FSBO ad you have cut out from the local newspaper. Draw a large *T* on your flip chart. On one side of the vertical line of the *T* write the word *has*. On the other side of the vertical line write **unknown**. Ask for a volunteer to tell you items listed in the ad so you can write the information under the *has* side of your *T*. Once you have listed the features from the advertisement, ask the group if there are some features not listed that you as a real estate agent would want to know. These items will form a list of questions you will ask the FSBO when you make your call.

Step 6

Explain to the group that when they call an FSBO their goal should be to set up an appointment to preview the home and meet the FSBO in person. They should not try to make a sale over the telephone! Tell the group to develop charts like the one you drew up to help in asking owners a few questions about their homes not listed in their ads. Instruct them that after they introduce themselves and disclose that they are real estate agents, they should ask a couple of questions about the house and then ask for the appointment.

Step 7

Cover the following extra points about the FSBO process:

- Preview the home. Remind the agents to take notes as they preview the home, and make a point to not take up too much time from the owners.
- Ask about doing a comparative market analysis (CMA). (Explain what the CMA does). Most people will love to have you do this. Don't forget to take a few digital photos to use in your CMA, but remember to always get permission from the sellers before taking the photos.
- Give the FSBO a videotape explaining how to prepare a home for showing. Leave a package of microwave popcorn with your business card attached. This will provide you with a good follow-up opportunity with the FSBO.
- Send a thank you card after the first visit. This is a lost and forgotten gesture today and one appreciated by everyone.
- Stay in touch! Remind the agents to stay in touch with the homeowners after they deliver the CMA. Many FSBOs will not list their properties with the agent at that point, but eventually, if they are unsuccessful in selling their properties, they will turn to real estate agents for help. Normally, the FSBO will hire the agent that he or she felt comfortable with and who stayed in touch. This is the key to winning the FSBO. Tell them to make sure they don't annoy or bother the person too much about how the home selling process is coming along, just keep in touch!

Step 8

Ask the group for some ideas and ways to stay in touch with an FSBO after the first visit. Some ideas that might come up include *write a sample ad, prepare sample flyers with digital photos, make short phone calls to ask how everything is going, provide information on new sales and listings in the neighborhood, and send handwritten notes with news articles enclosed that the FSBO might seem interested in.*

Step 9

If time allows, ask for volunteers to share successful FSBO methods they have used. Or, you could continue this topic into next week's meeting and allow some of your better agents or those who volunteered to share their methods. Postponing a week will allow you to visit with the agents in advance and find out how they plan to explain their procedures. This will also allow you time to set up some rules and guidelines for their presentations so things do not get out of hand, and so there will be more structure to the FSBO methods illustrated.

Step 10

Hold up the paperwork again that you began the meeting with. Find the paperwork with the following information written on the page you prepared in advance on the flip chart, and which has been hidden from the group.:

- Understanding the paperwork: 30%
- Having the home ready for sale: 26%
- Pricing the property correctly: 19%
- Enough time to sell the property: <u>14%</u>
                                              88%

Remind the group that out of every 100 FSBOs surveyed in 2003, 88 of the respondents could have used our help. As real estate agents we can help them with the paperwork and pricing, provide ideas and tips to prepare the home for sale, and, of course, we will be able to invest the time to market and sell their real estate.

- Is there any reason we shouldn't call on FSBOs?
- Is there any true reason why they wouldn't want us to call on them?
- Based on the statistics and information provided today, do you think the FSBO has a need for us?

Remind agents that working FSBOs is a must and can be a great source of revenue if prospected right.

Tell the agents that if your company does not pursue the FSBO, someone else will. Encourage everyone to work this market segment year-round. Take the information learned from today's meeting and use it to make more money through prospecting FSBOs.

If time permits, discuss the latest "no-call" rules for your state. You can normally obtain this from your state attorney general's office.

Finish The Sales Meeting With This Quote:

"It takes as much courage to have tried and failed as it does to have tried and succeeded."
Anne Morrow Lindbergh (1906–2001), writer, wife of Charles A. Lindbergh

ADDITIONAL NOTES TO COVER DURING MEEETING

Expired Listings

**THEME: Discovering that the Reason an Expired Listing Didn't Sell
Could Have Been Something Simple**

ITEMS NEEDED:
- Blank paper
- Flip chart
- Sample reading handout found on resource CD

ESTIMATED MEETING TIME:
- 10–15 minutes

MEETING OBJECTIVES:
- To encourage agents to create action plans for calling
  expired listings regularly
- To develop a list of possible ways to contact expired
  listings
- To focus on the need to set up particular saved searches in
  their local Multiple Listing Service (MLS®) and report
  when new expired listings become available in their
  market area

MEETING APPLICATION:

Step 1

Ask agents to help you create a list of reasons a property may not sell, and write them on your flip chart.

Answers should consist of but not be limited to:

- Priced too high
- Poor location
- Property does not show well

Step 2

Give agents the handout from the resource CD and ask them to read the paragraph and count the number of mistakes contained in the sample reading.

> A listing that does not selll is not always price related. Sometimes the property is in a pooor location, it could be priced to high or worse yet, showes bad. Their might be much cluter throughout the house, Or the next door nieghbor could come over and help kill the deal everytime someone shows the property. Their are many reasons houses do not sell.

Ask the group to tell you how many mistakes they found in the reading assignment you just provided them. The list below shows the number of mistakes.

- *Sell* not *selll*
- *Poor* not *pooor*
- Could be *priced <u>too</u> high*
- *Shows* and not *showes*
- *Clutter* and not *cluter*
- No capitalization for the word *Or* (or)
- *Neighbor*, spelled incorrectly
- *Every time* spelled wrong
- *Their* should be *there*

Step 3

Ask agents how the previous exercise relates to the expired listing from either the seller's or the agent's perspective. Sometimes the most obvious problems can jump out at us for why a property does not sell. Many times though, the problem or problems might go unnoticed on the surface to you or me. However, when we can dig down a little deeper and analyze the property from the buyer's view, we might getter a clearer picture of why the property will not or has not sold.

Step 4

Using the list the group developed for why properties might not have sold, have agents get into groups of three or four and assign each group a reason a home did not sell. Have that group develop a sample marketing piece to use to explain this in a listing presentation to an expired listing homeowner. Have the group assign a spokesperson to describe how they would design this part of the presentation and how they might present it to the expired listing customer. Use the remaining time to listen to the various ideas and list any suggestions on the flip chart. If your group is small you could do this together. Encourage your agents to take notes and write down these ideas to set up their own expired listing presentations for future use.

Step 5

Below are a few general wrap-up questions:

- What normally happens when an expired listing re-lists with another agency? *The price of the property is generally lowered.*
- Do you think the expired listing is easier to work with than the normal seller who has not been exposed to the market? Why or why not? *Explain that one good advantage to working with expired listing clients is that they have already been exposed to the market, and are familiar with how the process works.*
- What would be a good way to approach the expired listing customer?

Step 6

Depending on your local Multiple Listing Service, MLS®, you might consider using the remaining time to explain (or have someone familiar with computers and the MLS®) how to set up a saved search to notify you when listings go off market in a particular subdivision or area of the community.

Encourage the group to work the expired listing market, and to understand this is another good way to prospect for new business. Remind your agents to always double-check through the MLS® records that the property is off market before contacting the expired listing owner. This is a clear violation of many state laws to contact a seller presently committed under contract with another agent.

Finally, remind your agents of the current "no-call" list in force in many states, and to use other avenues to contact these potential expired listing clients.

Finish the Sales Meeting With This Quote:

> *"I find that a great part of the information I have, was acquired by looking up something and finding something else on the way."* Franklin Pierce Adams (1881–1960) American columnist and author

ADDITIONAL NOTES TO COVER DURING MEEETING

PROSPECTING MEETING

3

Prospecting I

THEME: Learning What It Takes to Be Successful in the Real Estate Business

ITEMS NEEDED:

- Perennial or annual flower seed packets
- Printed labels from resource CD, or you may buy blank white shipping labels and add the text indicated in the steps
- Flip chart

ESTIMATED MEETING TIME:

- 10–15 minutes

MEETING OBJECTIVES:

- To help agents develop a list of how prospecting can lead to one-time results or repeat business
- To help agents learn ways to prospect for long-term results, creating perennials from their current customer and client database

MEETING APPLICATION:

Step 1

Pass out the perennial seed packets with a blank white shipping label available from the resource CD. (A template that will print on Avery® label sheets 5264 is included with the CD.) Labels should not be affixed to the seed packets at this stage of the meeting.

SOW:

AGENT HINTS:

Ask for a volunteer to define what a perennial is. Explain that the word *perennial* comes from Latin, meaning *perennis,* from *per* (throughout) + *annus* (year).

The Merriam-Webster online dictionary defines a perennial as present at all seasons of the year, and continuing without interruption.

Step 2

Ask agents the following questions:

- Have you ever sold a home to a client, only to learn that a year or two later that client used another real estate agent to sell that home? *Naturally. This has happened to every experienced agent.*
- Why might this have happened? *Several answers could emerge, but keep asking for questions and answers until someone says it's because he or she did not stay in contact with that client.*

Step 3

Ask for a volunteer to read the planting instructions or sowing instructions on the back of a seed packet.

Step 4

(Prepare on your flip chart in advance the sample copy below or one you might like to see carried out in your office for long-term repeat client results.)

Have agents place the blank shipping labels you provided over the backs of their seed packets. (*Note:* If you used the label from the CD the words *Sow* and *Agent Hints* are on the labels). If not, have agents write those words on their labels. *Sow* should be toward the top of the seed packet and *Agent Hints* roughly midway down the label. Have agents form groups of two or three and, using a blank sheet of paper, develop a set of instructions to write next to the words *Sow*, and *Agent Hints*.

After five or so minutes ask:

- What do you believe is necessary to achieve long-term positive results and gain repeat clients?
- What are some good hints that agents need to carry out to be successful in the real estate business?

Pull back the paper where you have written the following instructions:

Sow:

Agent Hints:

Step 5

Write in the groups' responses under the appropriate headings.

Step 6

Have agents write in the responses that they feel motivated to incorporate in their real estate business on the seed packets given to them at the beginning of the meeting.

Step 7

Wrap up the meeting with the following questions:

- Do you believe there is a formula or plan to success in the real estate business?
- Why or why not?
- If you were planting a garden, and you failed to follow planting and cultivating instructions, what would happen to your crop?
- If you planted our garden, followed all of the instructions, but never tended to the crop thereafter, what would happen to it?

Remind the group that to be successful in real estate we must follow the advice and suggestions of others who have harvested a good business before us. We can choose to be present at all seasons of the year, and continue without interruption, or we can plant seeds that will last only a season and come back no more.

The choice is up to you!

Finish the Sales Meeting With This Quote:

> *"All work is as seed sown; it grows and spreads, and sows itself anew."* Thomas Carlyle, (1795–1881) Scottish essayist, historian, and philosopher.

<u>ADDITIONAL NOTES TO COVER DURING MEEETING</u>

PROSPECTING
MEETING

4

Prospecting II

THEME: Discovering Why We Should Prospect. Or Why Not?

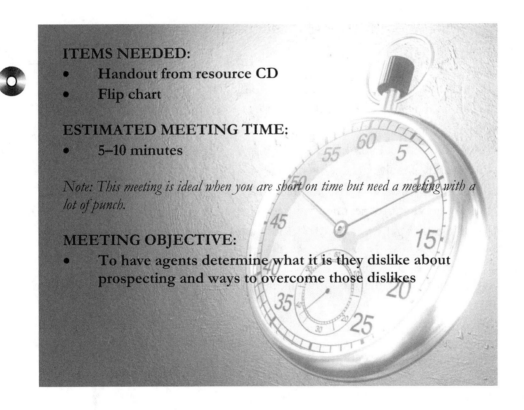

ITEMS NEEDED:
- Handout from resource CD
- Flip chart

ESTIMATED MEETING TIME:
- 5–10 minutes

Note: This meeting is ideal when you are short on time but need a meeting with a lot of punch.

MEETING OBJECTIVE:
- To have agents determine what it is they dislike about prospecting and ways to overcome those dislikes

MEETING APPLICATION:

Step 1

Distribute the following handout to the agents present:

Thoughts About Prospecting

Prospecting can mean different things to different real estate agents. Circle the responses that reflect your feelings on prospecting, and underline the ideas you feel are appropriate to other real estate agents you know.

- I don't know enough about prospecting to go out and do it.
- I hate to be turned down by people.
- I am afraid people will be rude to me.
- I don't need to prospect; I already have enough business.
- Most people don't like to be bothered, so I refuse to prospect.
- Most of my business is by referral.
- I don't have enough time to prospect.
- All of the good subdivisions are already taken in my office.
- It's illegal to prospect in my area.
- I don't like to talk to strangers.
- I don't want to be a high-pressure sales associate.
- I tried it once and got no results.
- I tried it once and messed up.
- I love to prospect and do it every day.
- Prospecting is only for new agents.
- A good agent does not have to prospect.
- I'm not good at prospecting, so I had better let someone else in the office do it.
- I would rather get my leads off of floor time.

After a few minutes, allow the group to talk about their responses and how they feel about prospecting.

Step 2

Share the following questions with the agents.

- Is prospecting essential to being a successful real estate agent? Why or why not?
- What is a good time to allot to prospecting on a daily basis?
- When is the best time of the day to prospect?
- Should prospecting be directed only toward new clients?

Step 3

Allow the group to share their most successful prospecting campaigns during their real estate careers.

Encourage everyone to prospect daily!

Finish the Sales Meeting With This Quote:

> *"Most men have worried about things which never happened, and more men have been killed by worry than by hard work."* Grenville Kleiser (1868–1953) American writer best known for humor, inspiration, and positive thinking (five books)

ADDITIONAL NOTES TO COVER DURING MEEETING

Scripts for Buyers

THEME: Using Phone Scripts When Working with Buyers

ITEMS NEEDED:
- Flip chart

ESTIMATED MEETING TIME:
- 10–15 minutes

Note: This is a good sales meeting idea when you are running short on time and preparation, and would like to involve the team with participation and development of the meeting.

MEETING OBJECTIVES:
- To have agents help one another develop some good scripts to use daily in their phone conversations with potential buyers
- To help agents learn the importance of role-playing with their scripts, and why practicing scripts daily is essential

MEETING APPLICATION:

Step 1

Ask the group to take a few minutes and list the top five questions they face from buyers when showing property.

Let the group divide into groups of three or four, talk about their top five concerns, and develop a list of possible good scripts (responses) to go with these concerns. After agents have a few minutes to record their answers, ask for feedback and summarize the results on your flip chart.

Use this time to talk about the various topics or problem areas that often arise when working with buyers.

Step 2

Ask for two volunteers to come forward and take part in a role-playing exercise with you. Explain to one agent that he or she will be a real estate agent and the second will be a buyer/prospect. Have the buyer play the role of a first-time homebuyer who would like more information about something a friend had mentioned briefly, and which entails talking with a real estate agent. The agent will need to explain a little about buyer's agency and why it would be good for the first-time homebuyer to use the services of a buyer's representative.

This is a good time for you to make sure the agents cover the normal points of interest your company policy has on buyer representative roles. It is also good to cover areas such as agency, disclosure, compensation, and anything else you want your agents to include when performing the role of buyer's agent and discussing this role with the buying public.

(You might want to prepare a checklist or recap form to pass out after this role-playing exercise. You can use this checklist with the agents to ensure that each area of your company policy and procedures for working with buyers were covered.)

When the role-playing exercise is finished, thank the agents and ask for positive, useful criticism that you can discuss as a group. List items the agents should incorporate into their presentations in this situation, and review your checklist to make sure it complies with the responsibilities of a buyer's representative.

Step 3

Ask the following questions:

- Are we more persuasive by memorizing great scripts and having quick responses to every issue, or should we just concern ourselves with our listening skills?
- Would it be helpful to have an outline prepared and memorized in explaining various aspects of our business to buyers?
- A good script should be how long to effectively address a question about how buyer's agency works?

Step 4

If time permits, and if you had a topic or two developed from the breakout sessions earlier, ask for volunteers to present (or discuss as a group) possible scripts to use when confronted with one of the issues.

Step 5

Ask the group the following questions:

- What is a good way to focus your attention on listening to your client's needs?
- Is it a good idea to repeat the question back to your client?
- If so, why? *Normally, this will show the other party that you are concerned about the question, and that you want to make sure you understand what this or her needs are before answering the question.*
- Should you repeat every question given you? *No, this technique can be over used, and should be handled with caution*

Encourage the group to share any other good suggestions or ideas they might have to help with listening skills.

Step 6

Remind agents that it is important to develop and practice good scripts for their day-to-day activities. This is a good way to help pass the time when they are driving in their cars or going for a long walk. Encourage them to think of possible situations or reflect on problem areas they face, and think of good responses to those circumstances.

Finish the Sales Meeting With This Quote:

"Practice makes perfect!" Unknown, but used often!

ADDITIONAL NOTES TO COVER DURING MEEETING

PROSPECTING
MEETING

6

Scripts for Sellers

THEME: Using Phone Scripts When Working with Sellers

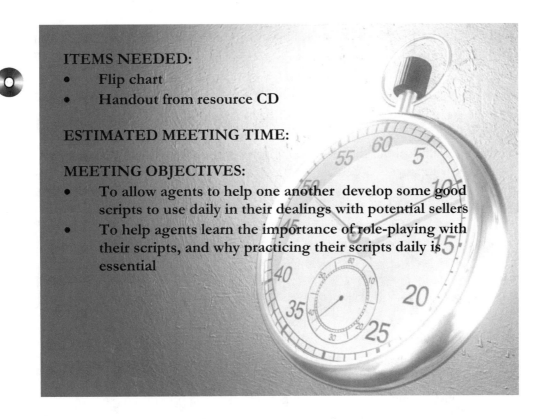

ITEMS NEEDED:
- Flip chart
- Handout from resource CD

ESTIMATED MEETING TIME:

MEETING OBJECTIVES:
- To allow agents to help one another develop some good scripts to use daily in their dealings with potential sellers
- To help agents learn the importance of role-playing with their scripts, and why practicing their scripts daily is essential

MEETING APPLICATION:

Step 1

Ask for a volunteer to come forward and engage in a role-playing exercise with you. Explain to the agent (out of the hearing of the group) that he or she will be a real estate agent and you will be a for-sale-by-owner (FSBO). The agent is to call you on the telephone and try to get an appointment to visit with you. You had a bad experience with a real estate company in the past and feel you can sell the property on your own. You have tried to sell the property for nearly two months on your own, and have had lots of lookers, but no buyers. The one ad you placed in the newspaper did not cost you much money, but you feel it generated a large number of buyers to look at your house, so you still feel you can do this on your own. If you can sell your home you plan to buy a bigger home for your family. (*Note*: You can ask for a second volunteer to play the part of the FSBO if you choose to not do this at your meeting). Begin the role-playing session by directing the agent to call the prospect.

Step 2

After the role-playing session, thank the participants, and explain to the group the role the FSBO was to play. Make sure the following areas were covered by the agent:

- Did the agent ask the FSBOs where they plan to move to when they sell their home?
- Did the agent ask how long they have tried to market their property?
- Did the agent touch on the issues of why many buyers looked at the property, and whether any of these buyers were not qualified to buy the home?
- Did the agent discuss how many would-be lookers could be warded off by qualifying callers?
- Did the agent ask about the marketing efforts of the previous sales associate or brokerage company?

Be sure to cover all the possible scenarios. Also, encourage the agent who took part in the scenario that if he or she missed several key points not to become discouraged, but to recognize the need for developing good scripts.

Step 3

Ask the group the following:

- What is a script?
- Why would a real estate agent want to develop a list of scripts?
- Should you memorize scripts?
- How detailed should you get with scripts?

Step 4

Use the next example with two more volunteers. You will need one of the volunteers to play the role of the sales agent, and one person to play the seller who has agreed to list a piece of property. The seller would like to price the property about $15 to $20 thousand dollars higher than your suggested list price. Have the seller use the sample dialogue and ad lib forward.

> **SELLER**
> "We would like to go ahead and list our home, however, the price you suggested is just too low. Let's start about $20,000 more than your figure."

After finishing the role-playing session, thank the volunteers and talk about what went right or wrong with this session. Encourage others to share ideas they have used to get price reductions.

Step 5

The next role-playing session will involve paying a full commission. The seller would like to list with the agent, but does not want to pay the commission rate your office is charging. The agent will need to explain why he or she cannot deviate from this rate and why the seller should pay the full marketing fee. The two volunteers will use the beginning script below and then role play the balance of the session.

> **SELLER**
> "I would love to let you sell my property, but only if you will reduce your commission. Your competitor has agreed to do it for less, and I think you should too."

When they are finished, thank the participants. Now use your flip chart to make positive points addressed by the agents. This is a good time to remind agents of anti-trust issues and to stay away from price fixing.

Extra role-playing issues outlined below will work during your meeting if time and volunteers permit. An alternative to the role-playing session is to allow agents to form groups of two or three and provide them with a case scenario as described with this meeting. Let them develop a sample solution as to what they would say if they were in one of these situations. The groups can share their responses. If you use this method, do only one example at a time, and then discuss this script before moving on to the next scenario.

Step 6

Other possible role-playing scenarios:

- Would like to list, but for a shorter time frame than your company allows
- Does not want a *For Sale* sign in the yard
- Must be present at all showings
- Wants listing left out of the Multiple Listing Service, MLS®
- Needs possession of property until they can move into their new home
- Complains that your company is not advertising the property every week
- Says that you have not showed the home one time in the two months listed
- Questions why he or she should lower the price after only two months
- Says he or she will take that offer if you lower your commission

- Thinks that you should lower your commission since it's been less than a week since listing, and the property is now under contract

Step 7

Remind agents how important it is to develop and practice good scripts in their day-to-day activities. Encourage them to think of possible situations or reflect on problem areas they were recently faced with, and have them think of good responses to those circumstances.

Finish the Sales Meeting With This Quote:

"And herein lies the secret of true power. Learn, by constant practice, how to husband your resources, and concentrate them, at any moment, upon a given point." James Lane Allen (1849–1925) American novelist, school and college teacher

<u>ADDITIONAL NOTES TO COVER DURING MEEETING</u>

Working the Technology-Savvy FSBO

**THEME: Discovering Alternative Ways to Find FSBOs
(For-Sale-By-Owners)**

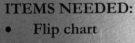

ITEMS NEEDED:

- **Flip chart**
- **Projector for your computer**
- **Laptop computer**
- **Live access to the Internet**

Note: If you do not own or have access to any of the previous three items, you can still accomplish this sales meeting idea by visiting the listed web sites in this agenda and printing out hard copies of the web pages to copy and distribute to your agents.

ESTIMATED MEETING TIME:

- **15 minutes**

MEETING OBJECTIVE:

- **To provide alternative ways for agents to work For-Sale-By-Owners (FSBOs) in today's real estate market**

MEETING APPLICATION:

Step 1

Brainstorm a few ways that agents obtain leads for listings. Write down the responses on your flip chart, or, if you do not have a flip chart, encourage each agent in attendance to keep a list of all ideas discussed by the group. The list should include things such as sphere of influence, for-sale-by-owners, expired listings, etc. After enough time has elapsed, explain to the agents that there is a new way to obtain leads without leaving their homes or offices. Better yet, the prospective clients will provide you with their names, phone numbers, and addresses.

Step 2

If you can project this exercise on a screen via a projector and laptop, go out on the Internet and visit the following site: http://www.owners.com. Once at this site, click on the state drop-down box and find your location. Follow this procedure on the following page by narrowing your choice down to the county in which you live. Submit your response and you should see a list (the area of the county your office is located in will naturally determine the number of leads) of for-sale-by-owners by price, city, etc. By clicking on the hyperlink to each listing, you can then pull up additional information about each property, including the owner's' names and how to contact them. *(A note for those without access to a live Internet connection or any of the other technology devices: You will want to visit this site in advance and print out this page showing the for-sale-by-owners index in your area. You may also want to click on one of the available links and print out detailed pages for the agents in attendance. Having a hard copy of the web sites you are talking about helps drive home the point in your presentation.)*

There are a couple of points to make when visiting these sites that will give your agents ideas about approaching these for-sale-by-owners. First, take notice of how many of these properties have pictures. Sometimes many of the listings will have numerous photos. This is a great way to explain to your agents the importance of having a lot of photos on each of their listings. If the listings do not have photos in their classified ads, you can explain to the agents that one good way to approach these prospective clients would be to offer to take digital photos for free and upload them to the for-sale-by-owner site for them.

Another good thing to look for is the ad copy the owner listed on the web site. If the ad copy is very good—and most of the time it is—explain to your agents how writing descriptions about their listings should not be taken lightly. Most homeowners wanting to sell their homes can write stunning ad copy for sites such as http://www.owners.com. The flip side to this suggestion is that, if the ad copy is weak or not much is mentioned, the agents can use this avenue in a professional and tactful manner to help the for-sale-by-owner rewrite some of the ad copy. Finally, point out to the agents how you can save your search so that you will be notified by e-mail for any new listings posted to the site. With this feature, new FSBO listings added to http://www.owners.com will be forwarded right to their e-mail inboxes.

Step 3

Below is a sample e-mail script that you can provide to your agents for ideas on how to approach the FSBO listings. It is a good idea to save this type of e-mail script in a folder on your hard drive for easy retrieval to copy and paste inside e-mails to send to prospective clients.

"Hi, my name is John Mayfield, and I am with Mayfield Real Estate in Farmington, MO. I noticed your ad on the Internet and wanted to give you some important information. First, please understand that in no way am I trying to discourage you from selling your house on your own. I think this is a good idea and occasionally it does work. What I did want to help you with is with a disclosure rule that some sellers are not aware of that pertains to lead-based paint. There is a federal law that requires all sellers, landlords, and agents to disclose the presence of lead-based paint to prospective clients with respect to housing built *prior* to 1979. If your house was built on or after this date, then do not worry about this information. However, if your home was built before 1979, you might want to check out the link below that will give you all of the information you need to know about this disclosure. I have copied a short paragraph right off the EPA's web site, which shows just how severe this law can be.

What if a seller or lessor fails to comply with these regulations?
A seller, lessor, or agent who fails to give the proper information can be sued for triple the amount of damages. In addition, they may be subject to civil and criminal penalties. Ensuring that disclosure information is given to home buyers and tenants helps all parties avoid misunderstandings before, during, and after sales and leasing agreements.

My training at Mayfield Real Estate allows me to be on top of the latest legal and environmental changes that are facing sellers such as you. Whenever I can help another individual with this information I love to pass it along. With our "sue-happy" world you never know when that next problem could arise right in our own backyard regarding lead-based paint and a failure to disclose. Click on the link below to visit this web site, and obtain the proper forms to use when you are ready to prepare a contract for a potential buyer. If you need any additional information please feel free to call me at 573-756-0077 or e-mail me at http://wwwjohnm@mayfieldre.com. I will be glad to help in any way I can.

http://www.epa.gov/opptintr/lead/leadbase.htm

Thanks for your time and good luck in selling your home. I will let the other agents in the office know about your home in case someone has a client looking for a home that matches your description.

By the way, I would love to preview your home. Call me if this would be possible.

John

John Mayfield, GRI, ePRO, ABR®, ABRMSM
Broker Owner - Mayfield GMAC Real Estate
Helping Families Since 1978!
Farmington, MO Ph: 573.756.0077 Fax: 573.756.1336
Web Site: http://www.mayfieldhomes.com

Have the group think of other types of e-mail letters that they could send to FSBO's via the Internet.

Step 4

Additional sites you could view for the meeting can be found by doing a general search using the words for-sale-by-owner. You could also try your local newspaper web site, which will normally have a classified section with many FSBOs posted. The main thrust to get across to your agents is the fact that they have many leads right at their fingertips with very minimal effort. In fact, once they have their systems and searches saved, the only thing they will need to do is check their e-mail on a daily basis!

Step 5

Using your flip chart draw a large circle. Next, cut a small sliver out of this circle illustrating the portion that represents the small piece of the pie that is available to agents to work and obtain new business. Stress to the agents that the best part of this new way of prospecting can be done right from their offices in front of their computers. Remind them to look and think outside the box for ways to contact and build relationships with these new, online for-sale-by-owners. The potential is unlimited!

Finish The Sales Meeting With This Quote:

> *"The future belongs to those who believe, and the beauty of their dreams."* Eleanor Roosevelt

ADDITONAL NOTES TO COVER DURING MEETING

Legal
Meetings

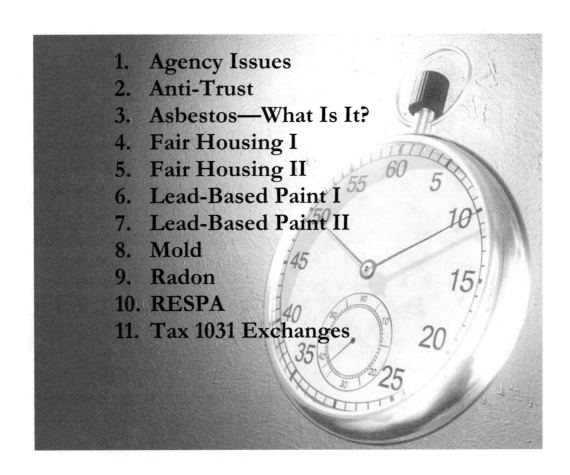

Agency Issues

THEME: Working with Agency Issues

ITEMS NEEDED:

- Blank paper
- Umbrella *(Optional—write or tape the letters "C.O.A.L.D." on various sections of the umbrella)*
- Flip chart
- Sample listing contract
- Sample buyer's agency agreement

ESTIMATED MEETING TIME:

- 15–20 minutes

MEETING OBJECTIVES:

- To remind agents of their roles and requirements when entering into an agency agreement with a consumer
- To ensure that agents understand the client/agent relationship created when buyers and sellers sign an agreement

MEETING APPLICATION:

Step 1

Write the following acronym on your flip chart:

C   O   A   L   D

Assign the agents into five groups and give each group one of the following titles:

> **C** ARE
> **O** BEDIENCE
> **A** CCOUNTING
> **L** OYALTY
> **D** ISCLOSURE

Step 2

Have each group brainstorm its assigned title, and list areas that, as real estate agents, they're responsible for when working with sellers. After several minutes bring the groups back and discuss the responses beginning with the word "care." Write the answers on your flip chart as topics come up.

Step 3
Client or Customer?

Hold up the sample listing contract, and explain that this listing contract creates a fiduciary obligation when signed by the seller. In other words, when a seller signs this agreement with your agent, an agency forms, and COALD is required from the agent and broker.

Hold up a sample buyer's agency agreement and ask the following questions:

- If a consumer signs a buyer's agency agreement, have the same agency responsibilities passed along to you as the agent? *Any time there is an agency created, the same fiduciary responsibilities apply.*
- Do you feel that one agency carries more weight than the other agency? *Remind the group that whether you are working as a seller's agent or a buyer's agent, COALD exists!*
- If a buyer chooses not to have representation, and does not sign a buyer's agency agreement, what would the buyer be in this transaction? *A customer, or third-party.*

Step 4

Ask the group the following questions and write their ideas and suggestions on your flip chart. (*Note: If your agency policy is unique to this subject matter, develop a list of questions that you need to cover with your group so that the agents understand and operate in accordance with your policy.*)

- Could you develop a checklist to follow ensuring that you use COALD with each client who signs an agency agreement with you?

Allow agents a few minutes to develop a sample checklist to refer back to when working with buyers and sellers. For example, what steps do you take after taking a new listing to fulfill the "care" responsibility of COALD?

- As an agent, what areas do you feel need polishing in regard to your fiduciary obligations to clients?
- Do you feel working as a buyer's agent is *always* the right decision? Why or why not?
- In two or three sentences, what is one way to describe your agency relationship to a potential client?
- What kinds of information must you keep confidential from a third party or another agent who is not working on your or your client's behalf? *Explain to the group that one good idea to remember is, if you would not tell the information if your client were sitting next to you, then don't say it!"*

Step 5

Hold up the umbrella you brought to the meeting, and open it up. Ask a volunteer to come forward to stand under the umbrella with you.

Explain to the group that the umbrella represents your fiduciary obligations to this client. Each area listed, COALD, is assigned to you as an agent, and it's your responsibility to ensure the client is protected and cared for during your agency agreement.

Remind agents that only a client, and no one else, is allowed under the umbrella! Whatever issues or problems arise, the agent must keep his or her umbrella of COALD in place for the client at whatever cost.

Remind agents not to forget honesty and accuracy to any third parties or customers involved in the transaction. But always, apply COALD to any and all clients!

Finish the Sales Meeting With This Quote:

> *"Whoever is careless with the truth in small matters cannot be trusted with important matters."* Albert Einstein (1879–1955) German-Swiss-American mathematical physicist, famous for his theories of relativity. *Ideas and Opinions of Albert Einstein* 1954

ADDITIONAL NOTES TO COVER DURING MEEETING

LEGAL
MEETING

2

Anti-Trust

THEME: Being Aware of Anti-Trust Issues

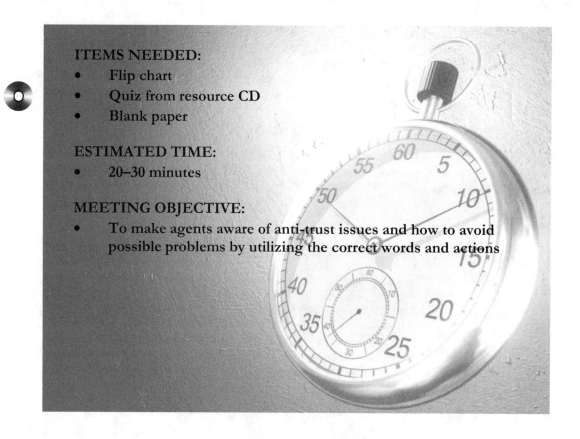

ITEMS NEEDED:
- Flip chart
- Quiz from resource CD
- Blank paper

ESTIMATED TIME:
- 20–30 minutes

MEETING OBJECTIVE:
- To make agents aware of anti-trust issues and how to avoid possible problems by utilizing the correct words and actions

MEETING APPLICATION:

Step 1

Pass out the following quiz and ask students to complete the questions with either *True* or *False*.

Answer the following questions either *True* or *False*.

1. _____ It is illegal to answer a telephone inquiry about commission rates, and use a statement such as "6% is the average/going rate."

2. _____ A company that refuses to restrict output, which in turn shrinks the supply of a product in a marketplace, is in violation of anti-trust.

3. _____ Real estate companies who refuse to show a competitor's properties, because that company offers a lower commission split, are in violation of anti-trust.

4. _____ If two companies in different market areas agree not to compete against each other in those market districts, this would constitute a violation of anti-trust.

5. _____ If all the real estate brokers in your community got together and agreed not to open on Saturdays, this could be a violation of anti-trust.

6. _____ If a specific area had only two brokers, and they got together and agreed to raise prices, this would be acceptable, as anti-trust violations always require three or more businesses to conspire to fix prices.

7. _____ It is okay to have preprinted forms that already include the commission rates and splits for your local board association.

8. _____ A board association can publish its own buyer's guide and provide discounts to its members as long as the board has complete control over the publication.

9. _____ Even a casual conversation about commission rates and splits could lead to the possible filing of an anti-trust suit.

10. _____ If someone asks you what fee your office charges, and then queries whether that rate is normal or average for the area, a good response would be to say that you know only what your own company charges for commission rates.

After agents have had time to consider the questions, discuss the answers (given below):

1.	True	6.	False
2.	True	7.	False
3.	True	8.	True
4.	True	9.	True
5.	True	10.	True

Step 2

Have the agents break into groups of three or four and assign the following topics to them. Have the groups develop a sample case study (one-to-two paragraphs) along with five questions to answer. Allow the groups five-to-ten minutes to develop their case studies and questions.

Case Study 1: Dealing with price/commission fixing
Case Study 2: Dealing with commission splits
Case Study 3: Dealing with agreements as to other listing terms
Case Study 4: Dealing with boycotts

Step 3

After the groups have developed their sample case studies and questions, have them exchange papers with another group in the room. Each group should now have someone else's case study. Allow the groups another five minutes to read over the scenarios and questions. Each group should appoint a spokesperson to read their assigned case study questions and answers.

Step 4

Bring everyone back together. Call on the groups to share their case study questions, and then explain the answers their group agreed upon. Use this time to talk about the various issues with anti-trust. Write key points on your flip chart to recap at the conclusion of the meeting.

Step 5

Ask the group the following questions:

- Do you feel anti-trust issues are a serious violation? *Stress to the group just how serious anti-trust violations are. Explain that no one should take anti-trust lightly.*
- What should you answer a consumer who asks what the standard or normal commission rate is in your area? *You have no idea what anyone else charges. You know only what your office charges.*
- Can you get into trouble by boycotting another real estate agency? *Yes!*
- Should you discuss or talk lightly about commission splits with other real estate agents from other firms? *No!*

Ask the group for any additional comments or questions. Encourage the group to read more about anti-trust and to stay informed on this topic.

Finish the Sales Meeting With This Quote:

> *"Four innate sentiments dispose people to a universal moral sense. These are sympathy, fairness, self-control, and duty."* James Q. Wilson

ADDITIONAL NOTES TO COVER DURING MEEETING

LEGAL MEETING

3

Asbestos—What Is It?

THEME: Dealing with Asbestos

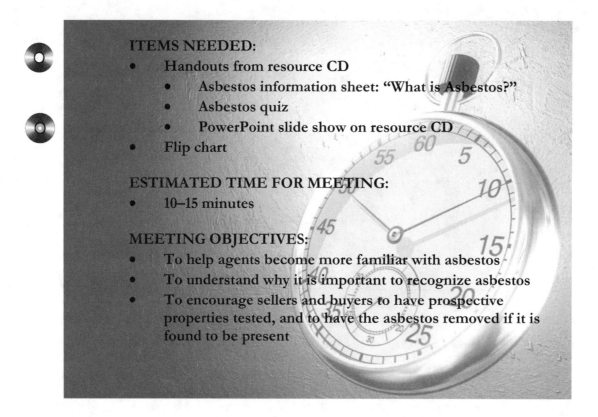

ITEMS NEEDED:
- Handouts from resource CD
  - Asbestos information sheet: "What is Asbestos?"
  - Asbestos quiz
  - PowerPoint slide show on resource CD
- Flip chart

ESTIMATED TIME FOR MEETING:
- 10–15 minutes

MEETING OBJECTIVES:
- To help agents become more familiar with asbestos
- To understand why it is important to recognize asbestos
- To encourage sellers and buyers to have prospective properties tested, and to have the asbestos removed if it is found to be present

MEETING APPLICATION:

Step 1

 Pass out the handout from the CD (reprinted from the EPA web site: "What Is Asbestos?"). Ask the agents to read this handout. When they have finished, pass out the quiz below for their completion. (While agents are completing this quiz, distribute a sheet with the information presented in Step 3).

Answer the following questions either *True* or *False*

1. _____ According to the handout, asbestos is a natural fibrous silicate mined for various material additives that are used for thermal stability, insulation, and tensile strength.

2. _____ To identify asbestos you would need to examine it under a microscope.

3. _____ Chrysotile, amosite, and crocidolite are the three most commonly found types of asbestos.

4. _____ When asbestos crystallizes, it takes the form of long thin fibers.

5. _____ The chrysotile form of asbestos is present in nearly 90–95% of all buildings in the United States today.

6. _____ *Amosite* is an acronym for "Asbestos Mines of South Africa," and is the second largest type of asbestos found in buildings in the United States today.

7. _____ Asbestos becomes a health hazard when disturbed and the small particles become airborne where individuals can inhale them.

8. _____ Researchers have still not determined what a safe asbestos level is.

9. _____ Depending on which of the three types of diseases asbestos can cause, the number of years the effects can go unnoticed in an individual range from 15 to 40 years.

10. _____ Asbestos-containing materials that become damaged may release dust particles into the air that can then be inhaled.

11. _____ The best course of action when dealing with asbestos in good condition is to leave it alone and monitor the condition of the asbestos over time.

Step 2

Go over the answers with the group with the added comments. Note that all answers are *true*.

Step 3

 Review the following points with the agents (included on the resource CD, "Facts to know about asbestos"). (These are included on the handout you distributed during the quiz.) Ask each person to read the information entitled "Where is asbestos in your home?" You may read these one at a time to the group or use the PowerPoint slide show.

- Most building products used today do not contain asbestos fibers. If a product does contain asbestos, it will be properly labeled.
- Many building products used before the 1970s contain asbestos. Some paint mixtures and joint and patching compounds contain asbestos. Drilling or sanding these products releases dust particles into the air that are dangerous when inhaled. The federal government banned the use of these products in 1977.
- A home built between 1930 and 1950 has a good chance of having asbestos in the insulation.
- Gas fireplaces with artificial embers and ashes contain asbestos.
- Some vinyl floor tiles and backings contain asbestos. Ripping up these older floors can release dust particles into the air that are harmful when inhaled.
- Many older steam pipes and furnace ductwork contain asbestos wrapping.
- Older products such as stovetop pads and ironing board covers contain asbestos material.
- Some older wall coverings, millboards, and floor coverings around woodstoves contain asbestos.
- Older furnaces (coal and oil) and their door gaskets contain asbestos insulation.

Step 4

Call for volunteers to read the sections entitled "What to do with asbestos."

- Normally, the best thing to do with asbestos that is still in good condition is to leave it alone.
- If asbestos is in good condition it is okay. Asbestos becomes a threat when disturbed and dust particles are released into the air.
- Always keep a close eye on any asbestos in your home. Make sure it does not begin to tear or look damaged. Watch for material that becomes water-damaged or has visible abrasions.
- If you notice any asbestos that has become even slightly damaged or disturbed, limit access to the area where the asbestos is and consult with a contractor on the proper removal of the asbestos. Be sure to check with your local health officials to find out where you can discard it.
- Always check to see if your house has asbestos before undertaking remodeling projects.

If you are able to prepare a list of qualified asbestos contractors in your area who inspect and remove asbestos, provide this list to your agents. Encourage agents to always avoid playing the role of inspector, and encourage them to get a qualified professional whenever in doubt.

Finish the Sales Meeting With This Quote:

"Health is the greatest of all possessions; a pale cobbler is better than a sick king." Isaac Bickerstaff (1735–1787) Irish playwright

ADDITONAL NOTES TO COVER DURING MEETING

LEGAL MEETING

4

Fair Housing I

THEME: Reviewing Fair Housing Guidelines
(Tenant Oriented)

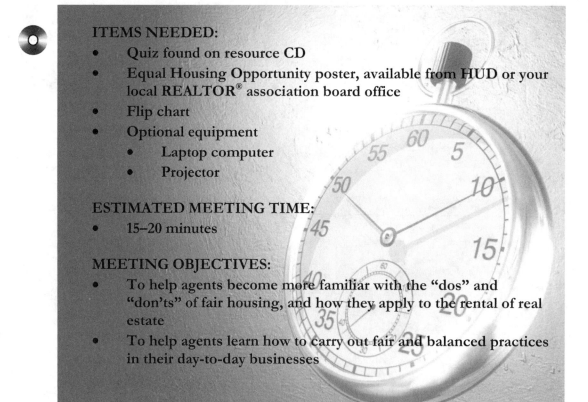

ITEMS NEEDED:

- Quiz found on resource CD
- Equal Housing Opportunity poster, available from HUD or your local REALTOR® association board office
- Flip chart
- Optional equipment
  - Laptop computer
  - Projector

ESTIMATED MEETING TIME:

- 15–20 minutes

MEETING OBJECTIVES:

- To help agents become more familiar with the "dos" and "don'ts" of fair housing, and how they apply to the rental of real estate
- To help agents learn how to carry out fair and balanced practices in their day-to-day businesses

MEETING APPLICATION:

Step 1

Pass out the following quiz and have the group complete it during the first five-to-ten minutes.

Fair Housing Quiz
Would the following statements be *Good* or *Bad?*

1. _____ "I'm sorry, John, but we really don't want alcoholics here. This even applies to people in a recovery program!"

2. _____ "Mary, I will need to see your medical records prior to making a decision about renting you this home."

3. _____ "I would love to rent to you, Mr. Neighbors, but unfortunately my insurance would go up dramatically if I did."

4. _____ "Mr. Smith, we do take younger children, but our policy prohibits teenagers. We feel the older children will disturb the other tenants."

5. _____ "Sorry Mrs. Adams, but a parent and child cannot share a bedroom at Riverwoods."

6. _____ "Sure, we do rent to families with children, Mr. Smith, but this does require an extra security deposit."

7. _____ "Our policy allows only for a maximum of three (3) people in a two- (2) bedroom apartment, Mrs. Lesh."

8. _____ "Mr. Smith, we do offer a building for couples with children, but unfortunately that building is fully occupied right now."

9. _____ "Sorry, Mr. Neighbors, our policy does not allow for pets. We haven't allowed anyone else to have a pet. Our policy even prohibits those people who might need a guide dog!"

10. _____ "Since you do not have anyone to take care of you, John, we will not be able to lease an apartment to you at this time."

Step 2

Review the quiz with the agents. All of the answers are *bad*.

Step 3

Ask the following questions:

- What are types of housing discrimination are illegal? *Answers: Any discrimination based on race, religion, ethnic or national origin, sex, age, familial status, or mental or physical disabilities.*
- Ask the group to identify some examples of possible housing discrimination they might remember from their pre-license real estate school days.
- Is it all right to set different rental and security deposits for different people who might inquire about a unit? *No.*

- Can a landlord refuse to allow a tenant to alter a unit or house if the tenant is disabled (provided the tenant puts the property back in the original condition before he or she leaves)? *No.*
- Can a landlord falsely deny that a unit is available when, in fact, there is an opening? *No.*
- Can a landlord run an ad that specifies "no children?" (Unless this is a senior housing project.) *No.*
- What do you tell someone who comes into your office and asks if you have anything for rent? *(Encourage your group to treat ALL consumers who enter your office the same. What you offer or do for one person or people you must do for EVERYONE.*
- What two protected classes were added most recently under the Title VIII Fair Housing Act? *Familial Status; and Handicap.*
- How many protected classes can be found under the Title VIII Fair Housing Act? *Seven. These are race, color, religion, national origin, sex, familial status, and disability or handicap.*
- What year did the Title VIII Fair Housing Act pass? *1968.*
- What year did the Civil Rights Act, which gave all citizens equal rights, originally pass? *1866.*

Step 4

Distribute copies of the Fair Housing poster, if available, to the group. Go over the poster with the group and continue to discuss the points of interest on the poster and from issues brought up during the meeting.

Step 5

Remind the group that discrimination will not be tolerated on any level in your organization, and anyone who does violate the company policy will be dealt with accordingly. (For most organizations this will mean immediate termination).

If your company has a company policy regarding fair housing, hand out copies from this section of the policy and review them with the group. If your organization does not have a fair housing compliance policy in place, implement one immediately, and then distribute copies of the policy to your agents and go over it with them.

Make sure you have the appropriate equal housing opportunity poster in place at all of your facilities in a location that can be seen by the general public. Review your advertisements and make sure the equal housing logo is present in all of your ads. If you have more questions or concerns, contact your local HUD office and discuss those issues and questions with them immediately.

You can conclude the meeting at this point, or you can proceed by combining the *Fair Housing II* sales meeting with this information to make one longer meeting. If you have other fair housing issues that you have noticed may be an issue on a local level, add those points here and allow time to discuss them with your group.

Finish the Sales Meeting With This Quote:

"We should not and cannot change all our differences. Each of us brings from our own background things which we should share. There is good in diversity." Georgie Anne Geyer (1935–) American foreign correspondent & syndicated columnist on foreign affairs. Newspaper clipping, Albert W. Daw Collection

ADDITIONAL NOTES TO COVER DURING MEEETING

LEGAL
MEETING

5

Fair Housing II

THEME: Reviewing Fair Housing Guidelines Further

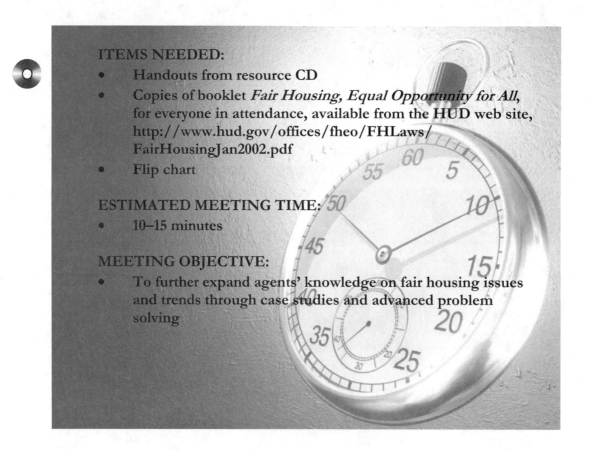

ITEMS NEEDED:

- Handouts from resource CD
- Copies of booklet *Fair Housing, Equal Opportunity for All*, for everyone in attendance, available from the HUD web site, http://www.hud.gov/offices/fheo/FHLaws/FairHousingJan2002.pdf
- Flip chart

ESTIMATED MEETING TIME:

- 10–15 minutes

MEETING OBJECTIVE:

- To further expand agents' knowledge on fair housing issues and trends through case studies and advanced problem solving

MEETING APPLICATION:

Step 1

Distribute the following case studies and questions and have the agents get into groups of three or four. Ask the agents to read the case studies and questions and discuss them with their groups.

CASE STUDY 1

Mary Lacy wants to rent a home on Main Street near a bus line since she has no transportation. Mary has a three-year-old boy. Landlord Larry thinks that renting his home to Mary would not be a good idea, because his apartment building is next to a busy highway, and his property is zoned commercial. Can Larry refuse to rent to Mary on this basis? Why or why not?

CASE STUDY 2

Joe and Cindy, an African-American couple, want to rent an apartment near Joe's work. Upon inquiring about renting in the complex, they are told that there are no units available. Shortly thereafter, Mike and Tammy, a white couple who pose as testers, visit the same apartment complex and are told there are units available, and are offered the opportunity to lease one. Has discrimination occurred? If yes, what portion of the Fair Housing Act has been violated?

Next, have the agents answer the following questions:

- What is blockbusting?
- Describe redlining.
- If a real estate agent were found guilty of "steering," what would he or she be guilty of?
- According to fair housing laws, you can never discriminate on what basis?
- What major Supreme Court case became grounds for striking down discrimination on the basis of race?
- What was the significance of the Civil Rights Act of 1964?
- What was added in 1974 to the Title VIII Act of the Fair Housing laws?
- What was added in 1988 to the Title VIII Act of the Fair Housing laws?
- The thirteenth amendment to the constitution did what for slavery?
- What is the significance of the fourteenth amendment to the U.S. Constitution?
- Explain what the Dred Scott Decision entailed.

- What is blockbusting? *Encouraging homeowners to sell their properties because of representations that there may be persons of a particular race or national origin moving into their neighborhood*
- Describe redlining. *Lending institution practice of denying or restricting loans in a particular area of a community*
- If a real estate agent were found guilty of "steering," what would he or she be guilty of? *Channeling home buyers to certain areas of the city or community*
- According to fair housing laws, you can never discriminate on what basis? *Race*
- What major Supreme Court case became grounds for striking down discrimination on the basis of race? *Jones vs. Mayer*
- What was the significance of the Civil Rights Act of 1964? *Prohibited discrimination in all federally assisted loan programs*
- What was added in 1974 to the Title VIII Act of the Fair Housing laws? *Sex*
- What was added in 1988 to the Title VIII Act of the Fair Housing laws? *Familial Status and Handicap*
- The thirteenth amendment to the constitution did what for slavery? *Abolished slavery*
- What is the significance of the fourteenth amendment to the U.S. Constitution? *Offered full citizenship and civil rights to African-Americans*
- Explain what the Dred Scott Decision entailed. *Blacks were denied U.S. citizenship*

Step 2

Review the answers with the group.

Step 3

Have the agents remain in their work groups and distribute copies of the booklet *Fair Housing, Equal Opportunity For All*, available from HUD. Ask each group to develop five true-and-false and five "fill-in-the-blank" questions from the booklet. When the groups have finished, have them exchange their questions with another group and then answer the newly created quiz. Allow five to ten minutes for this exercise.

Step 4

Go over the various quizzes that were created by the groups and allow the agents to share some of their questions and answers. Be sure to write any main points of interest that have not previously been raised.

Step 5

Have your agents turn to page two of the booklet *Fair Housing, Equal Opportunity for All*, and read the closing remarks from Mel Martinez, the 2003 Secretary of Housing and Urban Development (HUD):

> *Housing discrimination is not only illegal, it contradicts in every way the principles of freedom and opportunity we treasure as Americans. The Department of Housing and*

*Urban Development is committed to ensuring that for everyone seeking a place to live, **all** housing is Fair Housing.*

Remind the group that discrimination will not be tolerated on any level in your organization, and anyone who does violate the company policy will be dealt with accordingly. (For most organizations this will mean immediate termination).

If your company has a policy regarding fair housing, hand out copies of this section of the policy and go over it with the group. If your organization does not have a fair housing compliance policy in place, implement one immediately, and then distribute copies of the policy to your agents and go over it with them.

Make sure you have the appropriate equal housing opportunity poster in place at all of your facilities in a location that can be seen by the general public. Review your advertisements and make sure the equal housing logo is present in all of your ads. If you have more questions or concerns contact your local HUD office and discuss those issues and questions immediately.

Finish the Sales Meeting With This Quote:

"I have a dream that one day this nation will rise up and live out the true meaning of its creed: 'We hold these truths to be self-evident, that all men are created equal.'" Martin Luther King, Jr. (1929–1968) U.S. civil rights leader, orator, clergyman, youngest person to receive Nobel Peace Prize 1964. Speech, Washington, D.C., August 27, 1963

ADDITIONAL NOTES TO COVER DURING MEEETING

Lead-Based Paint I

THEME: Dealing with Lead-Based Paint Regulations

ITEMS NEEDED:
- Handouts located on resource CD for quiz
- Copies of the Lead-Based Paint disclosure form
- Optional items
  - *Lead-Based Paint, A Guide to Complying With The Federal EPA/HUD Disclosure Regulations*
  - Laptop computer and a projector

Note: You may order the booklet described above from the National Association of REALTORS® by requesting Item 141-558 (1/03). You may also visit the EPA web site at http://www.epa.gov and search for lead-based paint. The complete web site address as of this printing is http://www.epa.gov/opptintr/lead/

ESTIMATED MEETING TIME:
- 10–15 minutes

MEETING OBJECTIVES:
- To familiarize real estate agents with the lead-based paint disclosure laws
- To help agents become aware of the general lead-based paint definitions and terminology
- To make sure each agent present understands and can complete the lead-based paint disclosure form correctly

MEETING APPLICATION:

Step 1

Have agents complete the following three quizzes:

<u>QUIZ 1</u>

1. Who is responsible for informing sellers of their proper disclosure obligations?

   (a) Listing agent
   (b) Cooperating agent
   (c) Facilitator
   (d) Buyer's agent (receiving compensation from the seller)
   (e) All the above

2. The only agent free from the responsibility of disclosing to the seller information on lead-based paint is which of the following?

   (a) Facilitator
   (b) Cooperating agent
   (c) Buyer's agent (receiving all compensation from the buyer)
   (d) Listing agent
   (e) None of the above

3. Which of the following is exempt from lead-based paint disclosure?

   (a) Property sold at a foreclosure sale
   (b) Property that leased for 100 days or fewer and where no renewal or extension will occur
   (c) The buying, sale, or any servicing of a mortgage
   (d) Houses that have no bedrooms, and where the sleeping area is not located apart from the living space
   (e) All the above

Answer the following statements *True* or *False*

1. Housing intended for senior adults and housing where children under the age of six will **not** live are free from lead-based paint regulations. _____

2. When an existing lease renews and no proper disclosure is made to the lessee, no lead-based paint disclosure is needed. _____

3. All prospective buyers must receive disclosure of lead-based paint for target housing qualifying under the law. _____

4. Only the actual purchaser or lessee must receive disclosure from the seller, agent, or lessor about lead-based paint. _____

5. Sellers must allow buyers up to ten days to test for lead-based paint before the purchaser becomes obligated under the contract. _____

6. A purchaser may shorten or add time to the testing period for lead-based paint under the terms of the contract. _____

7. A seller cannot legally accept an offer to buy until the buyer receives the proper disclosures on lead-based paint. _____

QUIZ 3

Match up the following terms and definitions as defined in the booklet, *Lead-Based Paint, A Guide to Complying With The Federal EPA/HUD Disclosure Regulations.*

_____ Agent	A. Portions of a building generally accessible to all residents/users, including, but not limited to, hallways, stairways, laundry and recreational rooms, playgrounds, community centers, and boundary fences.
_____ Common Areas	B. 1) A surface-by-surface investigation to discover the presence of lead-based paint as provided by section 302© of the Lead-Based Paint Poisoning and Prevention Act (42 U,S.C. 4822) and; 2) The provision of a report explaining the results of the investigation.
_____ Inspection	C. Paint or other surface coatings that contain lead equal to or more than 1.0 milligram per square centimeter or 0.5 percent by weight.
_____ Lead-Based Paint	D. Any party who enters into a contract with a seller or lessor, including any party who enters into a contract with a representative of the seller or lessor, for selling or leasing target housing. This term does not include a purchaser's' representative who receives all compensation from the buyer.
_____ Lead-Based Paint Free Housing	E. Any entity that transfers legal title to target housing, in whole or in part, in return for consideration, including but not limited to individuals, partnerships, corporations, trusts, government agencies, housing agencies, American Indian tribes, or nonprofit organization. This term also includes 1) An entity which transfers shares in a cooperatively owned project, in return for consideration; and 2) An entity which transfers its interest in a leasehold, in jurisdictions or circumstances where it is legally permissible to separate the fee title from the title to the improvement, in return for consideration.
_____ Lead-Based Paint Hazard	F. Any housing constructed before 1978, except housing for the elderly or anyone with disabilities (unless any child who is less than 6 years old lives or is expect ed to stay in such housing) or any zero-bedroom home.
_____ Residential Dwelling	G. 1) A single-family dwelling, including attached structures such as porches and stoops; or 2) A single-family house unit in a structure that contains more than one separate residential dwelling unit, and in which each such unit is used or occupied or intended to be used or occupied, in whole or in part, as the residence of one or more persons.
_____ Target Housing	H. Any condition that causes exposure to lead from lead contaminated dust, lead-contaminated soil, or lead-contaminated paint that has deteriorated or is present in accessible surfaces, friction surfaces, or impact surfaces that would result in adverse human health effects as established by the appropriate federal agency.
_____ Seller	I. Target housing that has been found to be free of paint or other surface coating that contains lead equal to or in excess of 1.0 milligram per square centimeter or 0.5 percent by weight.

Answers to Quiz 1: (1) E, (2) C, (3) E
Answers to Quiz 2: All answers are *True*.

Following are the answers to Quiz 3:

D	Agent
A	Common Area
B	Inspection
C	Lead-Based Paint
I	Lead-Based Paint Free Housing
H	Lead-Based Paint Hazard
G	Residential Dwelling
E	Seller
F	Target Housing

Step 2

After agents have completed the exercises, review the answers with them and discuss areas of interest to the group.

Step 3

Distribute the sample lead-based paint disclosure form (this form is also found on the resource CD). Discuss the form with the group and go over the proper way for the form to be completed. Make sure that everyone knows how to fill out this form, and that everyone completes the form in its entirety!

Step 4

Combine Part II with this meeting if time permits, or conclude the meeting by instructing the group that you will have Part II of the Lead-Based Paint Disclosure Law next week.

Finish the Sales Meeting With This Quote:

"The real key to health and happiness and success is self knowledge." Unknown

ADDITIONAL NOTES TO COVER DURING MEEETING

Lead-Based Paint II

THEME: Working with Lead-Based Paint in Homes

ITEMS NEEDED:
- Handouts from resource CD
- Flip chart
- Copies of the pamphlet *Protect Your Family From Lead In Your Home,* offered by the EPA.

ESTIMATED MEETING TIME:
- 10–15 minutes

MEETING OBJECTIVES:
- To help agents determine where lead can be found in a home and how a family can check to see if lead is present
- To educate agents in ways that families can protect themselves from lead
- Finally, to provide a brief review for remodeling and renovating homes built prior to 1978, and how this relates to the Lead-based Paint Disclosure Act

MEETING APPLICATION:

Step 1

Give agents the following quiz:

Answer the following questions either _True_ or _False_.

1. Peeling, chipping, and cracking paint can all be factors contributing to high levels of lead in a home. _____

2. Areas that receive a lot of wear and tear, such as a porch and the handrails around the porch, are likely to be areas where lead-based paint is present. _____

3. Lead dust can become a problem when lead-based paint is heated. _____

4. When lead is present in soil, it can become a threat if it is brought inside by the tracking of shoes. _____

5. Just because a home has had lead-based paint in it does not mean the home will always be a hazard. _____

6. Blood tests for lead in children is especially important between the ages of 1 and 2. _____

7. Lead inspections can be done by visually inspecting a dwelling. _____

8. Testing of surface dust is another good way to inspect for lead. _____

9. When having a lead-based paint assessment performed on a dwelling, you should call the National Lead Informational Center and get a list of contacts in your area. _____

10. A renter does not have a ten-day right to inspect the property for lead. _____

Answers to the quiz are given below:

1.	True	6.	True
2.	True	7.	True
3.	True	8.	True
4.	True	9.	True
5.	True	10.	True

Note regarding Answer 10: _The ten-day testing option is not applicable to transactions involving a lease._

Step 2

Read the following information from the EPA web site "What You Can Do To Protect Your Family." Or, if you prefer, cut the bullet points into strips of paper and have various agents read the lead-based paint informational points.

What You Can Do To Protect Your Family

Taken from the EPA web site

http://www.epa.gov/opptintr/lead/leadinfo.htm#hazard

If you suspect that your house has lead hazards, you can take some immediate steps to reduce your family's risk:

- If you rent, notify your landlord of peeling or chipping paint.

- Clean up paint chips immediately.

- Clean floors, window frames, windowsills, and other surfaces weekly. Use a mop, sponge, or paper towel with warm water and a general all-purpose cleaner or a cleaner made specifically for lead. REMEMBER: NEVER MIX AMMONIA AND BLEACH PRODUCTS TOGETHER BECAUSE THEY CAN FORM A DANGEROUS GAS.

- Thoroughly rinse sponges and mop heads after cleaning dirty or dusty areas.

- Wash children's hands often, especially before they eat, before nap time, and before bedtime.

- Keep play areas clean. Wash bottles, pacifiers, toys, and stuffed animals regularly.

- Keep children from chewing windowsills or other painted surfaces.

- Clean or remove shoes before entering your home to avoid tracking in lead from soil.

- Make sure children eat nutritious, low-fat meals high in iron and calcium, such as spinach and dairy products. Children with good diets absorb less lead.

continued…

In addition to day-to-day cleaning and good nutrition:

- You can temporarily reduce lead hazards by taking actions such as repairing damaged painted surfaces and planting grass to cover soil with high lead levels. These actions (called "interim controls") are not permanent solutions and will need ongoing attention.

- To permanently remove lead hazards, you must hire a certified lead "abatement" contractor. Abatement (or permanent hazard elimination) methods include removing, sealing, or enclosing lead-based paint with special materials. Just painting over the hazard with regular paint is not enough.

- Always hire a person with special training for correcting lead problems— someone who knows how to do this work safely and has the proper equipment to clean up thoroughly. Certified contractors will employ qualified workers and follow strict safety rules set by their state or the federal governments.

- Contact the National Lead Information Center (NLIC) for help with locating certified contractors in your area and to see if financial assistance is available.

Step 3

Remind agents of the importance of complying with the lead-based paint disclosure requirements. Distribute copies of the lead-based paint pamphlet *Protect Your Family From Lead In Your Home*. If you do not have copies of this pamphlet available order some for your office, or visit the EPA web site at http://www.epa.gov/lead/leadpdfe.pdf to obtain a master copy. Discuss any questions someone might have regarding lead-based paint.

Encourage the group to read the pamphlet, and to make sure they are familiar with all of the aspects of conforming to the lead-based paint requirements studied during the meetings.

If anyone is still confused or needs additional help ask him or her to make an appointment with you to review the information again.

Finish the Sales Meeting With This Quote:

"He who has health, has hope; and he who has hope, has everything." Arabian proverb

ADDITIONAL NOTES TO COVER DURING MEEETING

Mold

THEME: Identifying and Managing Mold Contamination

ITEMS NEEDED:

- **Projector and computer**
    Note: Connection to the Internet would be helpful. If this is not available, you can visit the EPA's web site at: http://www.epa.gov/ebtpages/ airindoormold.html to print out more information for your agents
- **Quiz from resource CD**
- **Optional: laptop computer and projector**
- **PowerPoint slide show**

ESTIMATED MEETING TIME:

- **10–15 minutes**

MEETING OBJECTIVE:

- **To help agents become more aware of mold contamination and how it begins to grow in a home or building**

MEETING APPLICATION:

Step 1

(Research in advance a recent or related story on the devastation that mold can cause in a home, or on mold removal. If you have time, make copies to distribute to the group to discuss later in the meeting.)

Give agents the following quiz:

Answer the following questions either *True* or *False*.

Mold

1. Mold plays an important role outside a home but can be a threat when it begins to grow inside. _____

2. Most mold spores are invisible to the naked eye when floating through the air. _____

3. Mold will normally grow inside a dwelling when the mold spores land on a wet surface. _____

4. Mold always needs water to grow. _____

5. Mold can cause both allergic reactions and the release of toxic substances (mycotoxins) into the air. _____

6. Mold can cause symptoms in the lungs, eyes, skin, nose, and throat in both those who are mold-allergic and those who are nonallergic.

   _____

7. There is no way to get rid of all mold spores inside a dwelling.

   _____

8. If mold is present in a home the first course of action is to have the mold cleaned professionally. _____

9. The second course of action to address where mold is present in a home is to fix the water problem. _____

10. If a person cleans up the mold but fails to correct the moisture problem, the mold will probably return. _____

Go over the true/false quiz with your agents. All the answers are *true*.

Step 2

Hand out the document entitled *Ten Things You Should Know About Mold* taken from the EPA web site, and review the list with the agents.

Ten Things You Should Know About Mold

1. Potential health effects and symptoms associated with mold exposure include allergic reactions, asthma, and other respiratory complaints.

2. There is no practical way to remove mold and mold spores in the indoor environment; the way to control indoor mold growth is to control moisture.

3. If mold is a problem in your home or school, you must clean up the mold and eliminate sources of moisture.

4. Fix the source of the water problem or leak to prevent mold growth.

5. Reduce indoor humidity (to 30–60%) to decrease mold growth by venting bathrooms, dryers, and other moisture-generating sources to the outside; using air-conditioners and dehumidifiers; increasing ventilation; and using exhaust fans whenever cooking, dishwashing, and cleaning.

6. Clean and dry any damp or wet building materials and furnishings within 24–48 hours to prevent mold growth.

7. Clean mold off hard surfaces with water and detergent, and dry. Absorbent materials such as ceiling tiles that are moldy may need to be replaced.

8. Prevent condensation: reduce the potential for condensation on cold surfaces (i.e. windows, piping, outside walls, roof, or floors) by adding insulation.

9. In areas where there is a continual moisture problem, do not install carpeting (i.e., by drinking fountains, by classroom sinks, or on concrete floors with leaks or frequent condensation).

10. You can find molds almost anywhere; they can grow on almost any substance, providing moisture is present. There are molds that can grow on wood, paper, carpet, and foods.

If you have IAQ (Indoor Air Quality) and mold issues in your school, you should get a copy of the *IAQ Tools for Schools* Kit. There is more information on mold in the IAQ Coordinator's Guide under *Appendix H - Mold and Moisture.*[1]

Step 3 *(Optional)*

If you obtained and made copies of a story about the devastation that mold can cause in a home, or on mold removal, and have the time, distribute the copies to the group to discuss.

---

[1] Taken from the EPA web site, http://www.epa.gov/iaq/molds/moldresources.
htmlTen%20Things%20You%20Should%20Know%20About%20Mold

Finish the Sales Meeting With This Quote:

> *"When you arise in the morning, think of what a precious privilege it is to be alive—to breathe, to think, to enjoy, to love."* Marcus Aurelius Antoninus (121–180 A.D.) Emperor of Rome 161–180 A.D., distinguished Stoic philosopher

ADDITIONAL NOTES TO COVER DURING MEEETING

Radon

THEME: Identifying Radon Gas in Residential Homes

ITEMS NEEDED:

- Booklet from EPA entitled *Home Buyer's and Seller's Guide to Radon*
- An alternative to purchasing the booklets would be to visit the following web site and print copies as handouts for agents

    Web site address: http://www.epa.gov and search for "Radon"

- Printed color map from the EPA web site of your state and the county-by-county breakdown of risk level for radon http://www.epa.gov/iaq/radon/zonemap.html.
- Quiz handout provided below or on **CD ROM**

ESTIMATED MEETING TIME:

- 15–20 minutes

MEETING OBJECTIVE:

- To enable real estate agents to become more familiar with radon gas in residential homes

MEETING APPLICATION:

Step 1

Provide the following quiz to agents:

> **Answer the following questions either *True* or *False*.**
>
> 1. Most scientists believe that radon is not a threat to the general public. _____
> 2. Most radon testing machines are inaccurate and are in limited supply. _____
> 3. Testing for radon is difficult and requires a great deal of time if it is to be performed correctly. _____
> 4. Once radon is found in a home, it cannot be corrected. _____
> 5. Radon is found only in older homes. _____
> 6. Only certain areas of the United States are affected by radon. _____
> 7. A positive radon test in one home can generally determine if the homes next to it have radon, too. _____
> 8. Radon is found only in the air of homes and not the drinking water. _____
> 9. A home where radon was detected and later corrected is normally a hard home to sell. _____
> 10. If a person has lived in a home for a number of years and has had no side effects, testing for radon would be a waste of time. _____

Step 2

After participants have completed the quiz, go over the handout and discuss the correct answers.

1. **Most scientists believe that radon is not a threat to the general public.**

   FACT: Although some scientists dispute the precise number of deaths due to radon, all the major health organizations (e.g., the Centers for Disease Control and Prevention, the American Lung Association, and the American Medical Association) agree with estimates that radon causes thousands of preventable lung cancer deaths every year. This is especially true among smokers, since the risk to smokers is much greater than to nonsmokers.[2]

2. **Most radon testing machines are inaccurate and are in limited supply.**

---

[2] *Home Buyer's and Seller's Guide To Radon*. Environmental Protection Agency.

FACT: Reliable radon tests are available from qualified radon testers and companies. Active radon devices can continuously gather and periodically record radon levels to reveal any unusual swings in the radon level during the test. Reliable testing devices are also available by phone or mail order and can be purchased in hardware stores and other retail outlets. *Call your state radon office for a list of radon device companies that have met state requirements.*

3. **Testing for radon is difficult and requires a great deal of time to be performed correctly.**

   FACT: Radon testing is easy. You can test your home yourself or hire a qualified radon test company. Either approach takes only a small amount of time and effort.

4. **Once radon is found in a home, it cannot be fixed.**

   FACT: There are solutions to radon problems in homes. Thousands of homeowners have already lowered elevated radon levels in their homes. Radon levels can be readily lowered for $800 to $2,500. *Call your state radon office for a list of radon device companies that have met state requirements.*

5. **Radon is found only in older homes.**

   FACT: Radon can be a problem in all types of homes, including old homes, new homes, drafty homes, insulated homes, homes with basements, and homes without basements. Local geology, construction materials, and how the home was built are among the factors that can affect radon levels in homes.

6. **Only certain areas of the United States are affected by radon.**

   FACT: High radon levels have been found in every state. Radon problems do vary from area to area, but the only way to know the home's radon level is to test it.

7. **A positive radon test in one home can generally determine if the homes next to it have radon too.**

   FACT: Radon levels vary from home to home. The only way to know if your home has a radon problem is to test it.

8. **Radon is found only in the air of homes and not the drinking water.**

   FACT: While radon gets into some homes through the water, it is important to first test the air in the home for radon. If your water comes from a public water system that uses ground water, call your water supplier. If high radon levels are found and the home has a private well, call the Safe Drinking Water Hotline at (800) 426-4791 for information on testing your water. *Also, call your state radon office for more information about radon in air.*

9. **A home where radon was detected and later corrected is normally a hard home to sell.**

   FACT: In areas where radon problems have been corrected, home sales have not been blocked. The added protection could be a good selling point.

10. **If a person has lived in a home for a number of years and has had no side effects, testing for radon would be a waste of time?**

    FACT: You will reduce your risk of lung cancer when you reduce radon levels, even if you have lived with an elevated radon level for a long time.

Step 3

If you have obtained copies of the booklet *Home Buyer's and Seller's Guide to Radon*, hand out the booklets now and have agents go to the Radon Testing Checklist. Go over the items with your group.

Encourage anyone present who has had experience with a radon test or problem to share his or her story.

Close the meeting by reminding agents of the importance of our fiduciary responsibilities as agents for both buyers and sellers, and that encouraging radon testing would likely fall under this umbrella.

Finish the Sales Meeting With This Quote:

> *"There is nothing which we receive with so much reluctance as advice."* Joseph Addison (1672–1719) English author, politician, publisher, essayist, and poet

ADDITIONAL NOTES TO COVER DURING MEEETING

RESPA

THEME: Providing Agents with a Working Knowledge of the *Real Estate Settlement Procedures Act (RESPA)*

ITEMS NEEDED:

- Handout with the list of questions found in this section
- PowerPoint slides on resource CD

ESTIMATED MEETING TIME:

- 5–10 minutes

MEETING OBJECTIVES:

- To help agents become familiar with the Real Estate Settlement Procedures Act (RESPA)
- To encourage agents to report possible violations of RESPA to the appropriate authorities

MEETING APPLICATION:

Step 1

 Provide those present with a handout of the following questions from the resource CD.

REAL ESTATE SETTLEMENT PROCEDURES (RESPA) QUIZ

Answer the following questions either *True* or *False*.

1. A mortgage broker or lender must provide all borrowers with a booklet entitled *Settlement Costs and You* within three business days following a loan application. _____

2. A mortgage broker or lender is required to provide all borrowers a good faith estimate of closing costs within three business days following a loan application. _____

3. If a lender denies the borrower a loan within three days of an application, that lender does not have to provide any documents to the borrower. _____

4. The good faith estimate provided by the lender to the borrower must list the exact charges the borrower will incur on the day of closing. _____

5. A builder may agree to pay a portion of the buyer's closing costs or provide an upgrade package with the home provided the borrower uses its lender. _____

6. RESPA does not require the use of an escrow account by borrowers. _____

7. Closing costs could differ from lender to lender, which is one of the primary reasons behind the RESPA laws. _____

8. Lenders who require an escrow account must always keep a cushion, according to RESPA. _____

9. The HUD-1 Settlement Statement must be provided to the borrower one day before closing. _____

10. A borrower does not have to pay for charges that exceed the amount originally given with the good faith estimate provided by the lender. _____

Allow agents a few minutes to complete the quiz and then go through the list of questions and answers provided below:

REAL ESTATE SETTLEMENT PROCEDURES (RESPA) QUIZ

Answers

1. A mortgage broker or lender must provide all borrowers with a booklet entitled *Settlement Costs and You* within three business days following a loan application. *True*

2. A mortgage broker or lender is required to provide all borrowers a good faith estimate of closing costs within three business days following a loan application. *True*

3. If a lender denies the borrower a loan within three days of an application, that lender does not have to provide any documents to the borrower. *False*

4. The good faith estimate provided by the lender to the borrower must list the exact charges the borrower will incur on the day of closing. *False*

5. A builder may agree to pay a portion of the buyer's closing costs or provide an upgrade package with the home provided the borrower uses its lender. *True*

6. RESPA does not require the use of an escrow account by borrowers. *True*

7. Closing costs could differ from lender to lender, which is one of the primary reasons behind the RESPA laws. *True*

8. Lenders who require an escrow account must always keep a cushion, according to RESPA. *False*

9. The HUD-1 Settlement Statement must be provided to the borrower one day before closing. *True*

10. A borrower does not have to pay for charges that exceed the amount originally given with the good faith estimate provided by the lender. *False*

As with all sales meetings be sure to have the attendance record signed by your agents and record the topic "RESPA" under what was covered. You should also place a copy of the questions and answer sheet with this meeting planner in your file. It's important as a broker that you have good records to back up your proof of regularly covering real-estate related issues, such as RESPA, Lead-Based Paint, Fair Housing, etc.

Step 2

Ask the group if they have additional questions about RESPA. You might consider visiting the HUD web site and printing additional information regarding RESPA, or invite a local escrow agent to come and speak about RESPA requirements they face on a daily basis. As in previous sales meetings, assign topics to the groups and have them develop a list of sample questions from their assigned reading. After several minutes, have the groups exchange questions and answer the newly formed questions. Discuss the questions and answers with the whole group.

Step 3

Remind agents that we are never to cross the line and play attorney or other type of legal representative. All agents do need a working knowledge of applicable laws to guide their clients in the right direction if they notice or spot a violation in the law. Encourage agents to visit the HUD web site and read more about the RESPA. You can also go to http://www.hud.gov and search for RESPA or Real Estate Settlement Procedures Act.

Finish the Sales Meeting With This Quote:

> *"Keep true, never be ashamed of doing right; decide on what you think is right and stick to it."* George Eliot (1819–1880)

ADDITIONAL NOTES TO COVER DURING MEETING

LEGAL MEETING

11

Tax 1031 Exchanges

THEME: Familiarizing Agents with the Basics of 1031 Tax-Free Exchanges

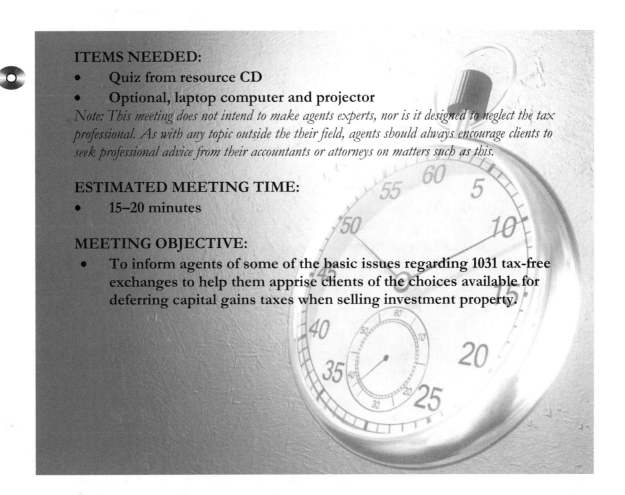

ITEMS NEEDED:
- Quiz from resource CD
- Optional, laptop computer and projector

Note: This meeting does not intend to make agents experts, nor is it designed to neglect the tax professional. As with any topic outside the their field, agents should always encourage clients to seek professional advice from their accountants or attorneys on matters such as this.

ESTIMATED MEETING TIME:
- 15–20 minutes

MEETING OBJECTIVE:
- To inform agents of some of the basic issues regarding 1031 tax-free exchanges to help them apprise clients of the choices available for deferring capital gains taxes when selling investment property.

MEETING APPLICATION:

Step 1

Distribute the following quiz and ask agents to complete it and find out how much they know about tax-free exchanges. Caution the group not to become frustrated or discouraged by the quiz if they do not know some of the answers. This meeting will help familiarize them with the basics of the 1031 Tax-Free Exchange laws.

Answer the following questions either *True* or *False*.

1. To complete a successful tax-deferred exchange, only two parties are necessary: a buyer and a seller. _____

2. Any tax liability deferred from a taxpayer using a Section 1031 exchange will eventually be repaid by the taxpayer's estate on his or her death. _____

3. *Basis* is the value or dollar amount of the property you own in the eyes of the IRS. _____

4. There is no need to use an escrow or closing agent to complete a Section 1031 tax-deferred exchange. _____

5. The money or other type of property given to one of the parties in a transaction to make up the difference between the exchanged values is referred to as *boot*. _____

6. The amount received by a seller minus his or her adjusted basis in the property is called the *gain*. _____

7. It is not uncommon for more than three parties to be involved in a tax-deferred exchange. _____

8. Any heirs to a parcel of real estate would receive a stepped-up basis in the value of the property if the deceased person had utilized the tax-deferred exchange program. _____

9. One disadvantage to using the Section 1031 tax-deferred exchange program is that no cash can be received at the time of the closing on the first property sale. _____

10. The party who acquires a property and then resells that same property for a fee during a 1031 tax-free exchange is called an *intermediary*. _____

11. Stocks, bonds, notes, and certain other forms of personal property do not qualify for tax-deferred exchanges. _____

12. For a tax-deferred exchange to be qualified, the properties exchanged must be what is deemed *like kind*. _____

13. All real property is considered *like kind*. _____

continued...

14. Under the like-kind rule, a commercial store building could be exchanged for raw land. _____

15. Under the like-kind rule, an apartment building could be exchanged for personal property. _____

16. For a property to qualify for a Section 1031 exchange, the property must have been held for a productive use in the trade or the business of the taxpayer. _____

17. A property purchased, remodeled, and then sold the following month could qualify for a Section 1031 exchange as long as the exchange was for like-kind property. _____

18. When the taxpayer relinquishes his property, he has 45 days (from the closing date) to name the replacement property he intends to purchase. _____

19. The taxpayer **must** close on the replacement property within 180 days of the date he or she relinquished the property involved in the exchange. _____

20. A taxpayer may transfer one or more properties under the exchange rules. _____

21. *Realized gain* and *recognized gain* are the two types of gains viewed in the eyes of the IRS for Section 1031. _____

22. *Realized gain* is the difference between the cash received (or other value) and the adjusted basis. _____

23. *Recognized gain* is the amount of the realized gain that the IRS would deem taxable. _____

24. *Boot* is the difference between the exchanged values given in cash or other property to one of the parties for his or her property. _____

25. If a mortgage or note is used for the difference between the exchanged properties, the terminology used to describe this scenario is called *mortgage boot*. _____

Go over the answers to the quiz (on the following pages) with your agents.

Answers to Quiz

1. To complete a successful tax-deferred exchange, only two parties are necessary; a buyer and a seller. *False. Under the 1031 tax deferred exchange, more than two parties are allowed.*

2. Any tax liability deferred from a taxpayer using a Section 1031 exchange will eventually be repaid by the taxpayer's estate on his or her death. *False. All taxes will be forgiven at this point; however the heirs will now own the property with what is called a stepped-up basis.*

3. *Basis* is the value or dollar amount of the property you own in the eyes of the IRS. *True. Show the following example on the flip chart. If a party purchased a building for $200,000, and made no improvements to the property, then the basis would be $200,000. Using another scenario, if the sellers had made no improvements, and the house had depreciated $10,000 over their ownership tenure, the basis would be $190,000.*

4. There is no need to use an escrow or closing agent to complete a Section 1031 tax-deferred exchange. *False. All tax-deferred exchanges require the services of an escrow agent. The sellers cannot touch any monies during the tax-deferred exchange.*

5. The money or other type of property given to one of the parties in a transaction to make up the difference between the exchanged values is referred to as *boot. True. This term is self-explanatory. Any difference between the exchanged properties is termed* boot.

6. The amount received by a seller minus the adjusted basis in the property is called the *gain. True. For Example, Seller A buys a property for $500,000. It depreciates $50,000 over her ownership period. Her basis is $450,000 if she has made no other improvements. The seller sells the property for $600,000. Her gain is $150,000.*

7. It is not uncommon for more than three parties to be involved in a tax-deferred exchange. *True. Examples of three parties in a transaction include a seller, buyer, and escrow agent.*

8. Any heirs to a parcel of real estate would receive a stepped-up basis in the value of the property if the deceased person had utilized the tax-deferred exchange program. *True. One advantage of a 1031 tax-deferred exchange is that the tax or gain is ultimately forgiven upon the death of the owner. The heirs would then have the property appraised and their basis would be the value at the time of the original owner's death.*

continued…

9. One disadvantage to using the Section 1031 tax-deferred exchange program is that no cash can be received at the time of the closing on the first property sale. *True. All cash must pass through an escrow agent and cannot be touched or received by the sellers.*

10. The party who acquires a property and then resells that same property for a fee during a 1031 tax-free exchange is called an *intermediary. True. Self-explanatory.*

11. Stocks, bonds, notes, and certain other forms of personal property do not qualify for tax-deferred exchanges. *True. Some personal property will qualify for a tax-deferred exchange, but for our basic understanding of exchanges only real property is considered.*

12. For a tax-deferred exchange to be qualified, the properties exchanged must be what is deemed *like kind. True. Like-kind means real property for real property A farm could be exchanged for a multi-family dwelling or vice versa.*

13. All real property is considered *like kind. True. For example , vacant land can be exchanged for rental property.*

14. Under the like-kind rule, a commercial store building could be exchanged for raw land. *True. Self-explanatory.*

15. Under the like-kind rule, an apartment building could be exchanged for personal property. *False. Self-explanatory.*

16. For a property to qualify for a Section 1031 exchange, the property must have been held for a productive use in the trade or the business of the taxpayer. *True. Tax-deferred exchanges are not allowed on personal dwellings.*

17. A property purchased, remodeled, and then sold the following month could qualify for a Section 1031 exchange as long as the exchange was for like-kind property. *False. For a tax-deferred exchange to occur, the property must be kept for a specified length of time. Normally, the IRS considers 12 months or longer to be the rule of thumb.*

18. When the taxpayer relinquishes his property, he has 45 days (from the closing date) to name the replacement property he intends to purchase. *True. A taxpayer can name up to three different properties he wishes to purchase during this 45-day period.*

19. The taxpayer **must** close on the replacement property within 180 days of the date he or she relinquished the property involved in the exchange. *True. This is very important. If the closing does not take place within 180 days, the taxpayer will be subject to a penalty and interest along with taxes due from the original sale of their property.*

20. A taxpayer may transfer one or more properties under the exchange rules. *True.*

21. *Realized gain* and *recognized gain* are the two types of gains viewed in the eyes of the IRS for Section 1031. *True. Realized gain is the difference between the cash you receive (or other value) and the adjusted basis.*

continued…

22. *Realized gain* is the difference between the cash received (or other value) and the adjusted basis. *True. Self-explanatory.*

23. *Recognized gain* is the amount of the realized gain that the IRS would deem taxable. *True. Self-explanatory.*

24. *Boot* is the difference between the exchanged values given in cash or other property to one of the parties for his or her property. *True. Self-explanatory.*

25. If a mortgage or note is used for the difference between the exchanged properties, the terminology used to describe this scenario is called *mortgage boot. True. Self-explanatory.*

Remind the agents again that this meeting did not intend to make agents experts, nor is it designed to neglect the tax professional. As with any topic outside the their field, agents should always encourage clients to seek professional advice from their accountants or attorneys on matters such as this.

Finish the Sales Meeting With This Quote:

"The art of taxation consists in so plucking the goose to obtain the largest amount of feathers with the least possible amount of hissing." Jean-Baptiste Colbert

ADDITIONAL NOTES TO COVER DURING MEEETING

Professional Development Meetings

1. Asking the Right Questions
2. Checklists
3. Customer Service
4. Don't Give Away Good Business!
5. Dress for Success
6. Education Benefits
7. Goal Setting
8. Group Problem Solving
9. Hats to Wear
10. Internet Basics
11. Investing in Your Career
12. Phone Image
13. Phone Tips
14. Playing It Safe!
15. Time Management

PROFESSIONAL
DEVELOPMENT
MEETING

1

Asking the Right Questions

THEME: Discovering How Asking the Right Questions Can Make All the Difference

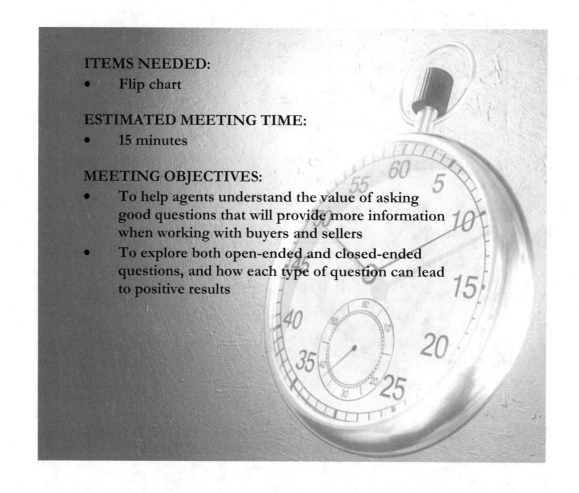

ITEMS NEEDED:
- Flip chart

ESTIMATED MEETING TIME:
- 15 minutes

MEETING OBJECTIVES:
- To help agents understand the value of asking good questions that will provide more information when working with buyers and sellers
- To explore both open-ended and closed-ended questions, and how each type of question can lead to positive results

MEETING APPLICATION:

Step 1

Have agents pair up and develop a list of questions that they would normally ask buyers in order to obtain information about the various issues listed below:

Buyer Answers Needed:

- Employment
- Down payment
- Price range
- Big or small house
- Current position, own or rent
- Working with another agent

After groups have had some time to go over the exercise, get everyone's attention and discuss the questions that each group developed.

Step 2

Now have the parties reverse their roles, and develop a list of questions they would normally ask sellers for answers to the following:

Seller Answers Needed:

- Why selling
- Where moving
- Pay-off amount
- Interested parties
- How arrived at price

After groups have had some time to go over the exercise, get everyone's attention and discuss the questions that each group developed.

Step 3

Ask the group the following questions:

- Open-ended questions are usually better than closed-ended questions. Why?
- What is a good example of a closed-ended question, and what does it usually achieve? *A closed-ended question needs either a yes, no, or a direct response from the intended party.*
- Open-ended questions should always begin with certain words. What are some of those words? *What, why, when, and how are good examples of beginning open-ended questions.*

Step 4

If the groups have broken up, reassemble them and give the following assignment. Groups will have three categories to work from:

- More Information
- Qualifying
- Building trust

Have the groups develop a list of open-ended questions to use for each of the above categories. After a few moments of working on this project, ask for responses and write those on the flip chart, while discussing answers with the group.

Step 5

Encourage agents to think about good questions to use when working with buyers and sellers, and to rehearse those questions when they are alone, for example in their cars or taking walks.

- Have them write questions they like and feel comfortable with in a journal to refer to for later use.
- Remind the group that preparation for asking the right questions at the right time is a critical role for the real estate agent!

Finish the Sales Meeting With This Quote:

"'How do you know so much about everything?' was asked of a very wise and intelligent man; and the answer was 'By never being afraid or ashamed to ask questions as to anything of which I was ignorant.'" John Abbott (1821–1893) Prime Minister of Canada

ADDITIONAL NOTES TO COVER DURING MEETING

 PROFESSIONAL DEVELOPMENT MEETING

2

Checklists

THEME: Making and Using Checklists

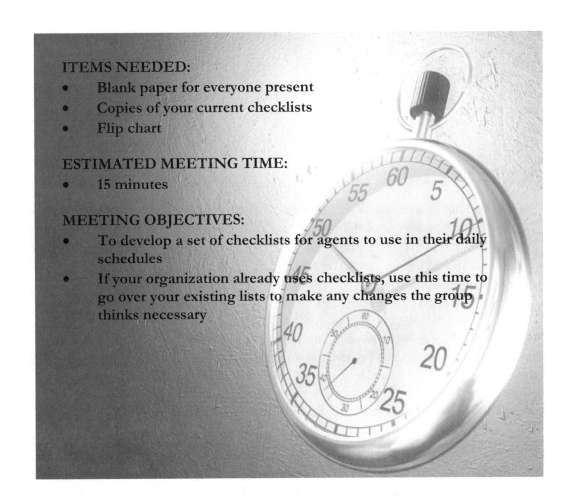

ITEMS NEEDED:
- Blank paper for everyone present
- Copies of your current checklists
- Flip chart

ESTIMATED MEETING TIME:
- 15 minutes

MEETING OBJECTIVES:
- To develop a set of checklists for agents to use in their daily schedules
- If your organization already uses checklists, use this time to go over your existing lists to make any changes the group thinks necessary

MEETING APPLICATION:

Step 1

Have agents get into groups of two or three each, and brainstorm the various types of checklists that would be valuable to the office. Some examples might be:

- Open House
- Pre-Listing
- Post-Listing
- Post-Offer
- Pre-Closing
- Post-Closing
- Working With Buyers
- First-Time Buyers
- Senior Buyers
- Investors
- Working With Sellers
- For-Sale-By-Owners
- Expired Listings
- Working with Seniors
- Other

List the various responses on your flip chart.

Step 2

Ask the whole group the following questions:

- You have just spent a full week at a hotel several states away from home. You are ready to check out of the hotel and your bags are packed. What do you normally do?
- You are an airplane pilot getting ready to take off for a cross-country flight. What will you do before you leave?
- You are about to have open-heart surgery. What would you like for the doctors and nurses to do before going into the operating room with you?

What do all of these issues have in common? They all need a good checklist for making sure everything's done correctly. Tell the group that today you will develop a new set of checklists for your office to use. If you already have a set of checklists in place, use this meeting as an opportunity to revise your existing checklists. Pass out copies of the checklists you are currently using for your group to review and discuss any possible changes.

Step 3

Assign one topic or checklist to each group. After five to ten minutes of discussion, have each group report on its checklists for each category. Write the responses for each category on the flip chart, or have one person from the group report the responses while someone else from that group writes the information on the flip chart. (*Note:* Use one sheet for each checklist category.)

Step 4

Finish the meeting by recapping some of the newly developed checklists. Ensure the agents that you will have the checklists typed and ready for distribution for next week's meeting.

Finish the Sales Meeting With This Quote:

> *"Progressiveness means not standing still when everything else is moving."* Thomas Woodrow Wilson (1856–1924) 28th president of the United States (1913-1921); president of Princeton University; Sponsor of League of Nations

ADDITIONAL NOTES TO COVER DURING MEETING

PROFESSIONAL DEVELOPMENT MEETING

3

Customer Service

THEME: Providing "Great" Customer Service

ITEMS NEEDED:

- Coffee, optional (three different pots of coffee, made with varying amounts of coffee in each pot)
- Flip chart
- Pickles for everyone

In advance, buy and read *Give 'em The Pickle*, by Robert E. Farrell with Bill Perkins, Legacy Communication (August 8, 1998). If your organization owns the video, incorporate it into your sales meeting. *(Note: The video is expensive, and may not be an economically viable option for everyone.)*

ESTIMATED MEETING TIME:

- 15 minutes

MEETING OBJECTIVES:

- To explain the various issues that make up great customer service
- To remind agents that it is sometimes the smallest details that can set us apart in bringing customers and clients for repeat business

MEETING APPLICATION:

Step 1

In advance, prepare three different pots of coffee, (optional). In the first pot use the amount of coffee that you would normally use for your regular meeting. Be sure to label the pot in some way so you know it is the "good" container. Prepare coffeepot number two with only one-fourth of the coffee that you would normally use. The coffee should look weak! For the third pot, use three times the amount of coffee you would normally use. Make it strong! Allow someone from the group to come forward and try a cup from each pot of coffee you have prepared. Ask the volunteer what is wrong with the three pots of coffee. The idea behind the coffee is to show the agents how our service should be consistent with each and every person we meet. Ask the group if they believe the services they provide the buying and selling public should differ like this coffee from client to client. Ask why.

Open the jar of pickles and pull one out and hold it up. Explain to the group that a man named Bob Farrell wrote a book (along with Bill Perkins) called *Give 'em The Pickle!* In a nutshell, the book is about customer service. Mr. Farrell explains that "the pickles" are the little or special items that we can do to make people happy!

Ask the group to brainstorm with you some ideas that your organization can do to make people happy. Begin with the seller's side of the transaction, and list items of importance to sellers that you are, or should be, doing to provide outstanding customer service. List the items on the flip chart, under the title of **Pickles for Sellers**. For fun, you might give or provide a pickle to each person who provides a suggestion.

Step 2

Now use a new sheet to brainstorm ideas for buyers. This time your flip chart should read **Pickles for Buyers**. Be sure to encourage the group to concentrate on the "little" business practices they can do. For example, suppose a prospective buyer, whom one of your agents has shown many homes to, buys a home from a for-sale-by-owner. The agent could provide that person postcards (with postage) showing a digital photo of his or her new home and a note telling friends and family of the address change. Even though the agent did not make anything off this transaction, that agent is being a good sport through the lost sale, and still providing a token of customer service. Tell the group that's a pickle!

Step 3

Title the next sheet on your flip chart **Pickles for Other Agents and Third-Party Vendors**. This portion of the training session is to display how our quality customer service should not just stop with buyers and sellers. Other agents can play a major role in whether our office is easy or difficult to work with in the eyes of other agencies. Third-party vendors for this exercise are lenders, title and escrow companies, appraisers, inspectors, insurance agents, or anyone else who might become involved in the sales transaction. Ask the group to list those small practices that we can do to help make third-party vendors' lives a little easier.

Step 4
Questions to ask the group before you wrap up the meeting:

- Why is customer service so important?
- Who suffers when customer service is poor?
- Is good customer service limited to only those individuals "outside" our organization?
- Does customer service need a commitment from everyone in the organization?
- What is one business practice you plan to do differently to provide great customer service?
- Should our customer service be the same quality for everyone?

Close with the story on why Mr. Farrell wrote his book, or another example of great customer service. In a nutshell, Mr. Farrell wrote his book because a customer had asked for some extra pickles at his business, and the employee for Mr. Farrell wanted to make a big ordeal about the request from the customer. Hence, Mr. Farrell's title and idea for his book was born, *Give 'em The Pickle.*

Remind the group that the customer is always right, and providing great customer service will pay big dividends for everyone in the organization.

Finish the Sales Meeting With This Quote:

"Do good to your friends to keep them, to your enemies to win them." Benjamin Franklin (1706–1790) American statesman, scientist, philosopher, printer, newspaper editor, and writer

ADDITIONAL NOTES TO COVER DURING MEETING

PROFESSIONAL
DEVELOPMENT
MEETING

4

Don't Give Away Good Business!

THEME: Building Clients for Life Not Just for a Single Transaction

ITEMS NEEDED:
- Flip chart
- Blank strips of paper

Note: Remind agents that any information they gather about their clients is for their use only and is not to be re-sold to outside vendors. Keeping clients' information private is extremely important in today's information-gathering society.

ESTIMATED MEETING TIME:
- 10–15 minutes

MEETING OBJECTIVES:
- To explain the need to build clients for a lifetime and not just for a single transaction
- To make agents aware of the importance of gathering good information about their clients and how to store and retrieve that data for future use.

This exercise helps the agents gain a better working knowledge about past clients, what their clients' needs are, and how they can better serve them in the years to come. All of this will, in turn, lead to more repeat business, as well as long-term trust and satisfaction between your agency and the client.

MEETING APPLICATION:

Step 1

List the following statistics on the flip chart:

- The average length a seller stays in a home today is approximately 5–7 years.
- The average time most homeowners keep a home loan with a lender before refinancing their mortgage or selling their home and paying the loan off is approximately four years or sooner.
- The average number of homes sold by an agent each year in our local area is _____ .
- According to *The 2002 National Association of REALTORS® Profile of Home Buyers and Sellers*, Chicago, IL: the percentage of people who used the same agent on their follow-up buy was approximately 40 percent.

Step 2

Explain to the agents that building clients for a lifetime is important in our business.

Ask the agents to write on blank pieces of paper the names of several clients they dealt with on a buying or selling transaction the previous year.

Next, ask agents to place a number next to each name representing the estimated number of times they have telephoned each of those clients since the closing. Stress to the group that they should list only the numbers that represent "personal" phone calls that were to follow up on how the clients were doing since the transaction.

Step 3

Now, have the agents write another number next to each name representing how many "personal" mailings they sent to that client. (*Note:* Encourage agents to not list weekly or monthly newsletters for this portion of the exercise. Stress the word *personal.*)

Step 4

Ask those agents who had to place a zero next to a client's name to raise their hands. Stress that it's okay if they listed a zero. Have the agents who raised their hands take their strip of paper and give it to someone else in the office. Mention that for every client they fail to get back with is being given to other real estate agents in their marketplace.

Step 5

Remind agents of these statistics from *The 2002 National Association of REALTORS® Profile of Home Buyers and Sellers*, Chicago, IL:

- Only 40 percent of homebuyers used their previous real estate agent when purchasing a second home.
- This means that 60 percent used a different agent for their next transaction.

Explain that one way to incur repeat business is through good record keeping after the sale, and by gathering the essential and needed data before closing, and then following up with those clients on a consistent basis.

Step 6

Break the group into pairs and ask them to brainstorm a list of information that would be helpful to get from your clients prior to or at the closing table. If your organization has a form it uses, review the form with the group. Ask everyone to list suggestions of items that should be on the form, and how this information could improve the company's long-term communication with clients. Have the groups also form a list of the types of correspondence and how often they feel information should be sent to clients "after" the sale.

After several minutes, ask the group to share their lists with the group. Write each point on the flip chart. Begin with one side of the transaction, such as from the seller's viewpoint, and discuss what information needs to go into a database, and how you could use that information to improve future communication with the seller. Then, do the same from the buyer's viewpoint .

If your company does not have a form to gather this information that the agent completes at the closing table, take the list you just developed with your agents and incorporate it into your closing practice. Develop a database so you can enter this information for easy retrieval in the future. Encourage agents to follow up with their clients regularly on a personal level.

Step 7

Tell the group that they can do one of two things:

1. Follow up with past clients and customers to win their business for a lifetime.
2. Give these prospects away, and allow other real estate agents to come along and profit off our leads.

The choice is ours.

Finish the Sales Meeting With This Quote:

> *"It's easy to stop making mistakes. Just stop having ideas."* proverb

ADDITIONAL NOTES TO COVER DURING MEETING

Dress for Success

THEME: Making a Good First Impression

ITEMS NEEDED:
- Stopwatch (or regular watch with second hand)
- Flip chart
- A food item, such as a cake. The front page of your local newspaper will work here too
- If you have any, print out two different e-mails that you have received in the last month or two that made an impression (positive or negative) on you

ESTIMATED MEETING TIME:
- 15 minutes

MEETING OBJECTIVES:
- To show agents how important first impressions are with the general public
- To explain the 30-second rule to agents
- To encourage everyone to dress professionally in their real estate careers

MEETING APPLICATION:

Step 1

Begin the meeting by starting your stopwatch and, at the end of thirty seconds, stopping it.

Step 2

Write **90 percent** on the flip chart.

Ask one or two volunteers to come forward and cut at least 90 percent of the food item away and separate the two portions from each other. If you chose to use the newspaper, have your volunteer cut away 10 percent of the paper, and then separate the portions.

Explain to the group that today's meeting is about dressing for success, or, more importantly, "creating a positive first impression." Be sure to stress that this meeting is not to poke fun at or embarrass anyone about his or her current dress style. This meeting is about true, hard facts that everyone will face daily. Many studies show that clothing covers about 90 percent of our bodies. We also have about 30 seconds to make a positive first impression with each client or customer we meet. During the first 30 seconds that we spend with someone, that person decides whether he or she likes us or not. Knowing these two facts, agents need to make sure that these issues are in tip-top shape.

Step 3

Have the group brainstorm ways we project an image daily to the various groups of people we meet. Write the ideas on the flip chart as each one is mentioned by the agents. Some ideas that should be mentioned include:

- Phone presence
- First contact with walk-in customers at the office
- Listing and showing appointments
- Open houses
- Local board of REALTORS® meetings
- Community and school functions
- Marketing efforts and daily correspondence, including e-mails

Step 4

After the group has finished, show a copy of an e-mail or letter (if you have one) you have received that did not make a good impression on you. Make sure to black out the names and any other information to avoid embarrassing the sender in front of the group. Briefly explain what your first impressions were. Now, share a copy of an e-mail or letter that made a positive, lasting impression after you read it. Explain to the group that to succeed in the real estate business we must make a positive first impression on our customers and clients. Remind the group that the image of their entire team is important. If one member of the team or organization portrays a bad image, it will affect the entire organization. Our clothing, appearance, and phone manners are all important if the team is to grow and prosper. Encourage the group to work together in making the image of the office and support members the best in the marketplace. Stress to everyone to use caution when making suggestions or talking to a team member about dress or other image issues. This is not an exercise in hurting others, or discouraging those who might be less fortunate or unable to buy new clothing at the time.

Then there are many sales associates who don't have a problem dressing for success, but have such bad phone manners that their successful attire won't have the chance to make any impression. It is, however, an opportunity for the agents to assess how they perceive that their images are projected through their clothing, appearance, and verbal communication skills. Then, they can decide how to improve that perception.

Remind the group that of all the issues we face as real estate agents, this is one area we can control. Our dress, attitude, and how we speak to others are all controllable for the most part. There might be agents who have physical or speech disabilities, which may limit them to a certain extent; still, all of us can exert some control over these issues by how our attitudes embrace these limits.

If your office has a company dress policy, go over the policy with your associates.

Finish the Sales Meeting With This Quote:

> *"There are some people who leave impressions not so lasting as the imprint of an oar upon the water."* Kate Chopin

ADDITIONAL NOTES TO COVER DURING MEETING

Education Benefits

THEME: Highlighting the Benefits of a Good Education

ITEMS NEEDED:

- Brochures or pamphlets about various real estate designations available to agents in your area
- Upcoming class schedules for educational events near your area *(Note: You can order most of these supplies direct from your local board of REALTORS® office or from the various agencies who administer and oversee these educational programs. You can also get most of this information right off the Internet. For a full listing of agencies and how to reach them go to http://www.realtor.org and search under the education tab)*
- One or more agents in your office who have earned a designation and proven to be a leader in the office. These agents will speak for a few moments on the value of their designations.
- Flip chart
- Projector
- Computer (if you plan to use the PowerPoint® slide show during the sales meeting)

ESTIMATED MEETING TIME:

- 10–15 minutes

MEETING OBJECTIVE:

- To encourage agents to further their real estate education through courses and seminars that might be available in your area

MEETING APPLICATION:

Step 1

Use the following quotes to begin your meeting, or copy the information on a separate sheet of paper.

- According to the data in the 2001 National Association of REALTORS® Profile 22 percent of all REALTORS® have earned the GRI designation.[1]
- According to the January, 1999 National Association of REALTORS® Profile those with such a designation earn over $18,900 more than non-designees, on an annual basis. [2]
- CRS Designees earn an average of $113,102 annually—three times as much as the typical REALTOR® who sells residential real estate. CRS General Members earn an average yearly income of $85,874—well above the average REALTOR® at $34,100.[3]
- CRS Designees complete an average of 45 transactions a year—three times as many as the typical REALTOR® agent—with average gross sales of $6.6 million yearly. CRS General Members average an even higher number of transactions—49—and have average annual gross sales of $6.3 million.[4]
- Roughly 64 percent of CRS Designees are women. CRS General Members are split almost identically: 63 percent women and 37 percent men.[5]

Step 2

Encourage agents in the office who've earned any designation to speak for a few minutes on what the designation has meant to them and their careers.

Step 3

Using your flip chart, ask the agents the following questions and write the responses on the flip chart.

- Why do you feel that continuing your education as a real estate agent is helpful?
- What benefits do you think arise from attending educational courses?
- What are some of the indirect benefits from attending educational classes as a real estate professional? *Answers here should include networking with other real estate agents and the benefit of future referrals.*
- Why else is education important as a real estate professional? *Risk reduction issues. Looks good on business resume.*

---

[1]http://www.realtor.org web site. Education/GRI/Why Become A GRI? January 20, 2003
[2]Ibid
[3]http://www.crs.com web site. Our Mission, History. January 20, 2003
[4]Ibid
[5]Ibid

Step 4

Encourage your agents to set a goal to take one new real estate class this next quarter. Suggest that some of the agents might sign up for a class or classes in groups. Many people find it easier to attend with others rather than alone.

If your company offers in-house training in various areas, encourage agent participation with those courses, too. Point out, though, that it is a good idea for agents to go outside the walls of the office to hear what others are doing in the real estate industry.

The networking that agents can do at workshops and classes is vital. You might provide some contest or scholarship backing for those who wish to take a course or attend a workshop. Have your assistant prepare a list of names for those who agree to take a course in the next three months and track the results.

Step 5

Pass out a schedule of courses in your area offered through program providers such as GRI, REBAC, CRS, CRB, and others, so the agents have this information readily available. You might note that this encouragement from you as the broker or branch manager at your weekly meetings will play a major role in agents seeking out education. Many agents may not agree to take part in more education at first, but if you keep talking up courses each week at your meetings, the idea will blossom over time. In fact, you might consider devoting a portion of your agenda to educational offerings for the coming month. Make sure that, throughout the year, you survey the progress of those who set goals to attend classes, and encourage them to fulfill that goal. Don't forget to announce any courses offered throughout the year.

Finish the Sales Meeting With This Quote:

> *"The roots of education are bitter, but the fruit is sweet."* Aristotle (384–322 B.C.)
> Greek philosopher, student of Plato, teacher of Alexander the Great

ADDITIONAL NOTES TO COVER DURING MEETING

Goal Setting

THEME: Setting and Measuring Goals

ITEMS NEEDED:

- One rock (medium sized rock to sit on a table)
- Velcro® dart board game with balls that stick to target surface
- Blindfold or large clean handkerchief to use as a blindfold
- Marshmallows
- Flip chart
- Blank paper for everyone in attendance

ESTIMATED MEETING TIME:

- 15–20 minutes

MEETING OBJECTIVES:

- To encourage agents to set goals, and to show the importance of writing their goals down
- To demonstrate to agents the proper way to set goals
- To demonstrate to agents the obstacles to goals
- To remind agents of the need to review their goals on a daily basis

MEETING APPLICATION:

Step 1

Have agents respond in writing as you ask them these questions:

- Write down three things you have always wanted to do in your lifetime, regardless of how crazy or silly it might seem.
- Why has this dream never become a reality? *To many it might be money, time, lost interest, etc.*
- Do you think you could reach these goals, and if so, what would you need to do to achieve these dreams?
- What one real-estate related goal would you like to achieve in your career over the next year?

Step 2

Have the group do the following:

- Beneath your real estate goal, write the word **Obstacles**. Write down all of the obstacles you can think of as to why you have not reached your goal.
- In another area write **Changes to Make** and write what you would have to do to achieve this real-estate related goal.

Step 3

Tell the group that goals are a big part of achieving dreams and desires in our lives. Explain that a Stanford study several years ago showed that nearly 80 percent of people who wrote their goals down, and looked at those goals every day, achieved those goals.

Another study by psychology researcher Michael Mischel, also from Stanford University, showed how being able to delay satisfaction and overcome the need for immediate results played a life-long effect on a person's character and his or her ability to achieve goals more effectively. In his study (from the early 1960s) Mischel provided each child in a group of four-year-olds with a marshmallow. The children were told that if they could wait for the researcher to return after running a quick errand, they could have two marshmallows. Only about one-third were able to wait for the researcher to return. The others took a marshmallow without waiting, thus demonstrating their inability to wait for a delayed satisfaction.

Mr. Mischel went back some twenty years later to interview the same test group, and found that most of the students from the one-third group, who waited for the delayed satisfaction, had better jobs and marriages, and seemed to be more successful with their lives than the others.

Step 4

Ask for a volunteer. Give the volunteer a ball for the dart game. Explain to the group that the "goal" for your volunteer is to throw the ball and hit the target. Place a blindfold on the volunteer and turn him or her around several times (be ready to help to avoid a fall). Ask the volunteer to now throw the ball. *It might hit the target, but it probably won't.*

Point out to your agents that setting individual goals, or not setting goals, is just like this exercise. If we do not set goals, our aim and throw have no direction or aim. Our days will be filled with throwing darts as if we are blindfolded.

Step 5

Now, focus the agents' attention on the rock. Ask the following:

- If you want to move this rock, what will you have to do?
- If you wanted to sculpt the face of a past president, what would you have to do?
- If you chose to do nothing with this rock, what will happen to it?

Remind the agents that the choice in life is up to us.

- We can have goals and haphazardly try to achieve those goals, like the blindfolded dart player.

- We can let the goals sit inside of us, just like this rock, and never move toward realizing our goals.

- Or, we can be like the children in the study, and understand that even though there is a price to pay for our efforts and endeavors, goals can come true. For us, the children's task seems so easy to accomplish. To a child, waiting for the delayed satisfaction was probably monumental, and did require a lot of effort to achieve.

Step 6

Explain to the group that, as adults, goals are important, if not vital.

Write **80 PERCENT** as big as you can on your flip chart.

Remind the group that this was the number from the Stanford study. On average, eighty out of every one hundred people who write their goals down and look at them daily achieve those goals.

Wow! Why not give it a try!

Finish the Sales Meeting With This Quote:

"You can't hit a target you cannot see, and you cannot see a target you do not have." Zig Ziglar (1926–) American master sales trainer, author, motivational speaker

ADDITIONAL NOTES TO COVER DURING MEETING

PROFESSIONAL DEVELOPMENT MEETING

8

Group Problem Solving

THEME: Developing Group Problem Solving

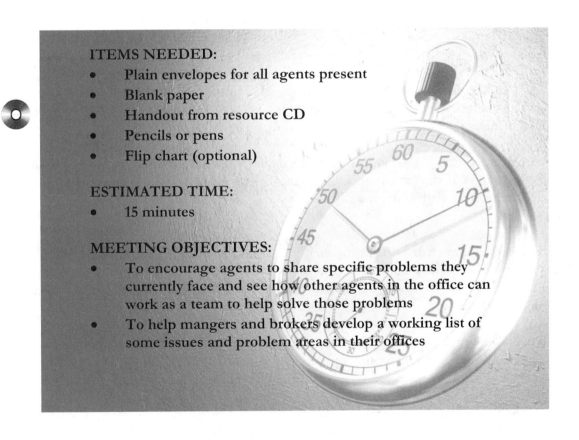

ITEMS NEEDED:
- Plain envelopes for all agents present
- Blank paper
- Handout from resource CD
- Pencils or pens
- Flip chart (optional)

ESTIMATED TIME:
- 15 minutes

MEETING OBJECTIVES:
- To encourage agents to share specific problems they currently face and see how other agents in the office can work as a team to help solve those problems
- To help mangers and brokers develop a working list of some issues and problem areas in their offices

MEETING APPLICATION:

Step 1

Hand out a pen, an envelope, and a piece of paper to each agent present.

Have agents write down specific issues that they are struggling with at the moment and give them the opportunity to seal up their problems in the envelopes. Now have agents swap envelopes with others in the room. Explain to the group that they have one of two choices:

- They can read the problem in the envelopes they have to their group.
  (Agents will break into groups in Step 2.)
- They can pretend to read the problem in the envelope, then ask for help in another area they presently face.

Remind everyone that all problems are to be taken seriously. Stress that this time is to be used on what areas the agents feel weak and unsure of in their real estate careers, i.e. phone tips, showing properties, etc. This is not a time to "bash" the office or anyone on the team.

Since every marketplace and area is different, develop a list of additional problems that you currently face in your office or marketplace. Seal the additional problems in envelopes and distribute with the listed problems above or at a different time to the group.

You may also wish to have agents write down one of their current problems or struggles as a new agent. After the group has listed their specific issues, have them place their paper responses inside the blank envelope and seal it up.

Below are some additional problems you can seal up in envelopes to distribute to the group for possible discussion. If you have other issues your office is facing, write those problems down and incorporate them with your group.

Problem 1: You have been trying to encourage a for-sale-by-owner to list with you, but after three or four visits, the prospect has still come up with excuses not to list. Discuss some ideas as a group on how you might approach the FSBO over the next couple of weeks without appearing too pushy.

Problem 2: As a new agent in the office you cannot get any appointments with potential clients. You feel uncomfortable asking for the appointment and need a guideline on what to say when a prospect calls in on a property. Develop a list or outline on how to approach this situation.

Problem 3: You have a listing that is very nice and in a great location. You receive calls daily on this home but everyone hangs up the second you disclose the price. You have discussed the price problem with the sellers but they want to wait a little longer before lowering their list price. What are some ideas on how you could approach the sellers about the price?

Problem 4: You're looking for a way to jump-start your real estate career. Your sales are good, and your listing inventory is acceptable, however you still feel as though your business is on a plateau and needs a boost. Discuss some ideas or ways to advance your career to a higher and more prosperous level.

Problem 5: You are a new agent in the office and have no idea where to begin your real estate career. List an outline on where to begin in developing a profitable real estate business. Group members who are established agents should suggest items they felt were beneficial as new agents or ideas they wished they had as new agents early in their real estate careers.

Step 2

Have the group break into groups of two or three and hand out envelopes for the group to read and discuss. Remind the group that this is an exercise to encourage and help each team player in the office with their problems. Make sure that everyone uses caution and care not to laugh or joke about any issue they receive. This is a time to work as a team, encouraging and helping one another with trials and issues others in the office are facing. After several minutes in which the groups discuss solutions to their assigned problems, invite the groups to share suggestions on how they would handle these issues. Explain to the whole group that if you cannot address all the questions, you will review the listed problems and work toward developing meetings to deal with those topics, or pick up next week where you left off today.

Be sure to visit the breakout groups as they open their envelopes to oversee what problems and issues come up, and to help facilitate group discussion and involvement.

Finish the Sales Meeting With This Quote:

> *"Success is sweet and sweeter if long delayed and gotten through many struggles and defeats."* Amos Bronson Alcott (1799–1888) American teacher, philosopher, writer, transcendentalist, reformer

ADDITIONAL NOTES TO COVER DURING MEETING

PROFESSIONAL DEVELOPMENT MEETING

9

Hats to Wear

THEME: Finding Out What Hats You Wear

ITEMS NEEDED:
- Five to ten different style hats (several inexpensive ball caps would be ideal, but any type or hat or cap will do)
- Strips of paper
- Safety pins
- Felt tip marker
- Flip chart

ESTIMATED TIME:
- 10–15 minutes

MEETING OBJECTIVES:
- To encourage your associates to define the number of hats they wear throughout the week
- To teach agents how to assign tasks and goals to those identified areas of their lives
- To show agents the need for weekly planning to help carry out their goals and tasks

MEETING APPLICATION:

Step 1

Ask for a volunteer to come forward. Ask this individual to list the various hats he or she wears throughout the day or week. For example, a woman might say mother, daughter, sister, MLS® chairperson, cancer society board member, girl scout troop leader, real estate agent, etc.

As your volunteer lists the various hats, write the responses on the flip chart.

Have someone else write the various responses on the strips of paper, and pin those slips to the hats you brought to the meeting. Be sure to include areas of interest or clubs and organizations the person serves on. The goal of this exercise is to list every role this person assumes throughout the week.

Step 2

After your volunteer has exhausted his or her list, ask the group to name any hats that they have to wear weekly that were not listed. Add the new responses to the list on your flip chart. If there are enough slips of paper, continue to have your volunteer write the responses and pin them to other areas of your hats.

Step 3

Explain to the group that whether we are aware of it or not, each week requires all of us to wear different hats. Unfortunately, some weeks we do not wear our various hats well or even put them on. For example, if you have titled one of your hats "sister," what have you done lately that would be beneficial to your sister? All of us wear a hat as a real estate agent, yet we may have gone an entire week without calling one of our clients.

Step 4

Display the hats to the group with the slips of paper pinned to them. Ask the group the following questions:

- What is an idea you could use to make each hat important throughout the week?
- Would weekly planning be helpful in wearing these hats? Why or why not?

Ask everyone in the group to think of one thing that would bring more meaning and satisfaction for each hat listed on the chart that he or she will be wearing this week. For example, for the real estate agent hat, sending a note or making a phone call to a client updating him or her on the marketplace would be a step in a positive direction in wearing that hat.

Step 5

Encourage the group to list one idea for each hat on the chart that would be worthwhile and add value to that area of their lives. As they write their goals down, remind them that each week offers a new beginning and new opportunities for them to succeed and move forward.

Tell the agents to visit with you at any time they need encouragement or extra help with the numerous hats they find themselves wearing.

Finish the Sales Meeting With This Quote:

"Go oft to the house of thy friend, for weeds choke the unused path." Ralph Waldo Emerson (1803–1882) American philosopher, essayist, poet, and lecturer

ADDITIONAL NOTES TO COVER DURING MEETING

PROFESSIONAL
DEVELOPMENT
MEETING

10

Internet Basics

THEME: Learning Internet Basics

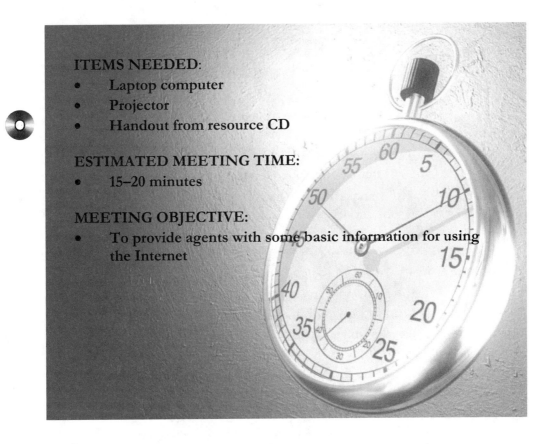

ITEMS NEEDED:
- Laptop computer
- Projector
- Handout from resource CD

ESTIMATED MEETING TIME:
- 15–20 minutes

MEETING OBJECTIVE:
- To provide agents with some basic information for using the Internet

MEETING APPLICATION:

Step 1

If you have a good technology person in your office who might want to lead this sales meeting, recruit that person in advance. A list of helpful suggestions can be found in Step 3. Hand out the quiz from the CD for the agents to complete to test their knowledge of the Internet.

<u>**Basic Internet Quiz**</u>
Answer the following questions either *True* or *False*.

1. _____ Resolution is a reference for the number of pixels displayed on a computer screen.

2. _____ The larger the screen resolution, the smaller the text will appear on the screen.

3. _____ If you make your screen resolution as large as possible, you can fit more information on the computer screen.

4. _____ IF YOU TYPE IN ALL CAPITAL LETTERS, IT APPEARS THAT YOU ARE SHOUTING TO THE PERSON READING YOUR MESSAGE.

5. _____ The symbol **:-)** refers to a smiley face.

6. _____ The symbol **:-D** refers to laughing.

7. _____ The symbol **:-o** refers to being surprised.

8. _____ The above symbols are called smileys, and referred to as emoticons.

9. _____ If you offend someone by e-mail or through posting a message to a newsgroup, it's called flaming.

10. _____ URL stands for Uniform Resource Locator, and designates the address for where a file is located on the World Wide Web.

11. _____ A URL will contain no spaces.

12. _____ A home page is the beginning point for any web page.

13. _____ To search for a particular topic, you could go to a web site such as http://www.google.com and type in the name of that topic. The site will then provide a list of places this topic is found on the Internet.

14. _____ According the NAR's latest member profile, 77 percent of REALTORS® use e-mail in their business.

15. _____ The Internet consists of hundreds of thousands of networks and millions of computers all connected around the world.

Step 2

Review the quiz with the group after they have had some time to complete the questions. All the statements are true.

Step 3

Give this list of suggestions to the person who has agreed to lead the meeting, or use it yourself:

- Explain further about URLs, and how agents can register their own domain names.
- Explain why it is necessary to have an e-mail address that advertises either the agent's web site or the company web site. For example, JohnM@MayfieldRE.com, looks much more professional than juicyfruit@hotmail.com, or john456712@aol.com. Also, explain how capitalizing certain letters looks better than using all lowercase in the address. For example, which of the two following addresses is easier to read? http://www.mayfieldre.com, or http://www.MayfieldRE.com.
- Explain how search engines work.
- Provide a list of the top search engines.
- Show how to set a home page in Internet Explorer and with Netscape.
- Talk about AOL and the differences between AOL web browsing and the traditional web browser.
- Explain the office's computer and Internet policy.
- If you do not have an Internet policy as to what agents can use the office computer equipment for, this is an excellent time to set up a policy and have everyone sign it. If your office has an Internet policy in place, go over the policy with the agents so they're reminded of the office rules concerning the use of technology in your company. Be sure to have everyone present sign the attendance roster so you can have a record of having covered this material in case a future violation arises in the office.

Step 4

Finish the meeting by encouraging agents who do not know much about using the Internet to take any classes available in the area. If you can research this in advance, find out where and when basic computer courses are conducted in your area, and prepare a list that includes costs and phone numbers to give out to your group. You might plan to have a class the following week on going over the MLS® online. Recruit someone within the office who knows how to do this, or has found some secrets using the MLS® online. Or you could ask the MLS® vendor if someone can be sent to your office to demonstrate how this is done.

Remind agents there will always be a faster, better way to do real estate work with technology; it just takes practice and persistence.

Finish the Sales Meeting With This Quote:

"If automobiles had followed the same development cycle as the computer, a Rolls-Royce would today cost $100, get a million miles per gallon, and explode once a year, killing everyone inside." Robert Cringely

ADDITIONAL NOTES TO COVER DURING MEETING

PROFESSIONAL DEVELOPMENT MEETING

11

Investing in Your Career

THEME: Investing in Your Career

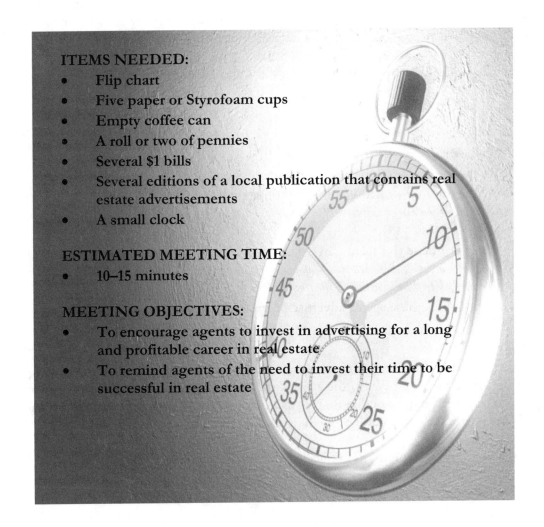

ITEMS NEEDED:
- Flip chart
- Five paper or Styrofoam cups
- Empty coffee can
- A roll or two of pennies
- Several $1 bills
- Several editions of a local publication that contains real estate advertisements
- A small clock

ESTIMATED MEETING TIME:
- 10–15 minutes

MEETING OBJECTIVES:
- To encourage agents to invest in advertising for a long and profitable career in real estate
- To remind agents of the need to invest their time to be successful in real estate

MEETING APPLICATION:

Step 1

Before the meeting recruit a couple of volunteers and give them an equal amount of pennies with instructions to place the pennies in the small cups when you ask them to do so. Each cup should be labeled with the appropriate agent's name. Explain to the group that today's meeting is about money and time. Place five cups on a table in front of the group, along with a coffee can wrapped with a sheet of paper on which the words **Future Profits** have been written.

Step 2

Have the group split up into groups of three or four. Ask the groups to look through the magazines and make notes on who the people are who have advertised in the publication, and how many ads they have.

Instruct the groups to list additional marketing efforts that some of the agents listed in the magazine have done that they have noticed; for example, billboards, postcards, cinema ads, or other promotional ideas. After the groups have had some time to make notes, call the group to order and ask for volunteers to list the advertising agents they found and which of their marketing activities have been discussed. List these agents on the flip chart.

Step 3

Pose the following questions to the group:
- Who are some of the larger advertisers?
- Are these larger advertisers also top agents in our board?
- List the top four or five agents in your marketplace. *Write the names on the flip chart for the group. If you can obtain this information in advance from your MLS®, do so, and distribute a copy to the group.*
- Are any of these top agents advertising in the magazine your group looked through? *If so, write a yes next to each name, and ask for the number of pages the top performing agent advertised on in the magazine. Write that number by each name.*
- Do you think these agents advertise because they know advertising is important?

Step 4

One at a time, have each agent with pennies come forward and place the money in the cup with his or her name on it. Explain to the agents that what each volunteer is doing is what most agents do on a year-in, year-out basis. They take the profits they make from their transactions and fail to realize the importance of building lasting relationships with their clients.

After the first agent with pennies has finished, call for the second agent assigned with pennies to do the same thing with his or her cup. Proceed with this plan until all of the pennies have been placed in the cups.

Step 5

Ask the final volunteer to come forward and begin placing the dollar bills into the coffee can, one at a time. While the dollar bills are being placed into the coffee can, remind agents that investing in their real estates career is vital for their continued growth and success in the real estate business.

Step 6

Encourage the group to glance back through the magazines one more time. As they glance through the publications, remind them that many agents will invest a large portion of their income in their real estate careers. Others will invest a small token and expect the same return.

Hand the cups with the pennies to the agents who volunteered for this part of the presentation. As you hand the pennies from the cups (one by one) to one of the agents, remind the agents that if this is what they invest in their careers, this will also be their portion of return.

Take the can with the dollar bills to the agent who helped with this role, and remove the dollars, handing them one at a time to the volunteer. Stress to the group that those who invest in their careers will earn more than those who invest nothing.

Remind the agents that advertising is not a "one-time" effort. Just because a particular ad or marketing idea does not work the first time it is offered does not mean it's a bad idea. Advertising takes time and patience to work effectively.

Step 7

Hold up the small clock you brought to the meeting. Explain that you want to conclude the meeting focusing on the second ingredient for investing in your career.

Write the word **TIME** on your flip chart.

Tell the group that they can spend all of the money they want on marketing themselves, but if they invest no time with their careers, they will go nowhere. Agents must be willing to invest the time to succeed in real estate sales.

Step 8

Write the following list on your flip chart on a separate sheet (also, you could have listed these on the flip chart prior to the meeting).

- If you worked four hours a week at a local retail store, how much pay would you receive?
- If you are building a new home, and spend 20 hours a week doing it, how long would it take you to complete?
- If you wanted to read a book with a large number of pages, and read only one or two pages a day, how long would it take you to finish the book?

Tell the agents that to be successful at any of these endeavors, they would have to invest much more time. Remind the group that the same principles apply to becoming a successful real estate agent. To accomplish great goals will require an investment of time and money in their careers.

Money and time are both essential ingredients in your real estate business. Because, after all, it is your business!

Finish the Sales Meeting With This Quote:

> *"Doing business without advertising is like winking at a girl in the dark. You know what you are doing, but nobody else does."* Stuart Henderson Britt quoted in the *New York Herald Tribune*, October 1956

ADDITIONAL NOTES TO COVER DURING MEETING

Phone Image

THEME: Perfecting the 30-Second Drill

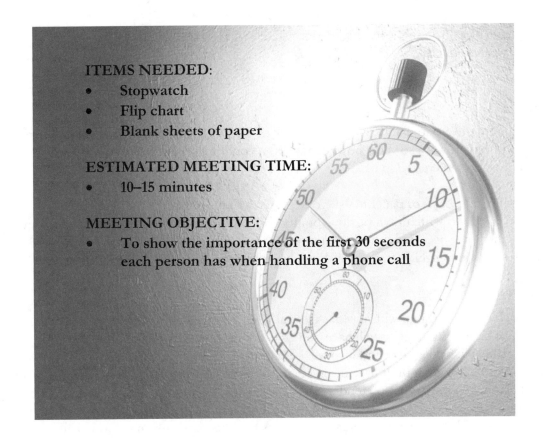

ITEMS NEEDED:
- Stopwatch
- Flip chart
- Blank sheets of paper

ESTIMATED MEETING TIME:
- 10–15 minutes

MEETING OBJECTIVE:
- To show the importance of the first 30 seconds each person has when handling a phone call

MEETING APPLICATION:

Step 1

This sales training exercise will concentrate on a nonvisual image we present daily, and that is how we are perceived on the telephone, or our voices.

Ask the group the following questions:

- How important do you think a person's voice is in the real estate business? *Hopefully, you will hear answers about many of our leads coming via the telephone. Stress to the group that a large percentage of prospects come by way of a telephone call.*
- Have you ever called a business, not knowing who you were speaking to, but felt that there was something about this person that you did not like? *Most groups will have many who answer yes.*
- How quickly did you come to this conclusion about this person? *Most people normally decide this within the first 30 seconds.*
- Why do you think you had that sense of dislike? *Answers could include the person's attitude, manners, tone, verbiage used, etc.*

Step 2

Point out to the group that today's meeting will deal with the image we display daily when using the telephone. It will also show how the first 30 seconds can either make or break our ability to keep prospects interested in us.

Pass out blank sheets of paper to everyone present. Explain that the purpose of this exercise is for the agents to write down positive points about a house the office currently has listed, or homes they have been in during the last month that they liked. Stress that they are to write down only some of the highlights, and finish the list with the price.

Step 3

Ask each agent to pair up with another agent and tell that agent over the phone about the home he or she has chosen. Agents will have only 30 seconds to describe this home. Have the groups decide who will be the caller and who will be the agent, explaining that everyone will get to play both roles. Allow for a brief time of preparation before starting your stopwatch. The exercise will begin when the person pretending to call says, *"Hi, I'm calling about the house on XYZ Street. Can you tell me how much the price is?"* Begin the exercise, and, when the 30 seconds are up, tell the group to stop. Now have the agents switch roles, and begin the exercise again, calling "Stop!" when another 30 seconds have passed.

Step 4

Ask the following questions:

- Did the 30 seconds go by quickly?
- How much information were you able to provide in 30 seconds?
- How many of you introduced yourselves?
- How many asked for an appointment?
- What did you like about how your partner started the conversation?

Allow for other discussion that may come up with the group, then ask:

- Do you need more than 30 seconds for a drill like this? Why or why not?
- Do you think consumers will make a decision about you during the first 30 seconds of a phone conversation?
- What do you think a caller normally wants to know when he or she calls about a specific property?
- What kinds of questions are good to follow up with after you give the caller the price?
- Should you use closed or open-ended questions with the phone caller?

Mention that, whether we like it or not, 30 seconds is about all the time we have with most consumers. Most of our days are spent in 30-second snippets. Television and radio commercials normally come in 30-second blocks, most news stories are 30-second segments, and so on. Why? Tell agents to look again at the piece of paper on which they wrote their lists earlier. Call out "Begin" and have them stare at the paper and think about that house. After 60 seconds have passed, stop your watch and say, "Stop!" Ask the group how many people began to think about something else during that time span. Tell the group the time they just spent was only 60 seconds. Did it seem longer?

Step 5

Continue with this question:

- Does this mean we have to speak as fast as we can? *No.*

Write the word **SPA** on your flip chart. This word will be an acronym for a good reminder on how to deal with phone callers during the first 30 seconds. With any spa we normally think of relaxation. *SPA* will remind you to make the caller feel at ease; do your best, and to give that caller a good feeling about you. The *S* will stand for "Set the stage." The *P* stands for "provide/paint a picture of the property." And *A* represents "ask for the appointment."

Encourage your agents to use this acronym and remind themselves during every phone call to

- Smile—this always helps to set the stage.
- Paint a picture of what they are describing
- Ask for the appointment

Finish the Sales Meeting With This Quote:

"A man without a smiling face must not open a shop." Chinese Proverb

<u>ADDITIONAL NOTES TO COVER DURING MEETING</u>

Phone Tips

THEME: Practicing Phone Techniques

ITEMS NEEDED:
- Flip chart
- Telephone
- Blank pieces of paper
- One small mirror
- Two small wastebaskets

  Label one of the wastebaskets **Lost Opportunities**, along with a large **$** under this phrase. Name the other wastebasket **Company Profits**, with another large **$** underneath this phrase.

- Optional Equipment
  - Laptop computer
  - Projector

ESTIMATED MEETING TIME:
- 15–20 minutes

MEETING OBJECTIVES:
- To encourage agents to understand the importance of each and every phone call that comes into the office
- To help agents understand that each phone call represents a dollar value regardless of what or whom the call may be for
- To help agents identify the types of phone calls that the office might field each day
- To teach agents the appropriate way to respond to each call

MEETING APPLICATION:

Before the meeting, recruit a top producer or someone you feel does an outstanding job with property phone calls to give a brief outline on how he or she fields incoming calls. Ask the volunteer to list his or her main points, and write those responses on the flip chart. Thank the volunteer, then ask for other ideas or comments on taking phone calls.

Step 1

Begin the meeting by stating the phrase that you would "prefer" each agent to use when answering the telephone. For example, "Good Morning, XYZ Realty, my name is John, how may I help you?" Another greeting that is starting to gain popularity at many businesses across the country is "It's a GREAT day at XYZ Realty! My name is John, how may I help you?"

Ask the agents questions about the following scenarios:

- Using the above example, let's say the caller asked for one of our agents, and I responded "Joan is out showing property, may I take a message for her or allow you to leave a message in her voice mail?" Is there a dollar value on that phone call?

- What if the caller were an appraiser asking if a property we sold last year had a basement or not? Would that call have a monetary value?

- Let's assume the caller told you at the beginning of the conversation that he was a next-door neighbor, and was curious as to the price of the new listing on his street. Is that caller worth money to the company?

- Finally, a caller noticed one of your advertisements, and was curious as to the location, price, or other information that might have been omitted from the ad about a property. Does this call have a dollar value associated with it?

The answer to all of the above examples is a resounding YES! Remind the agents that each and every call that comes into the office has the possibility of some type of monetary rewards associated with it, whether it be immediate or in the future.

Step 2

Ask the group to estimate the number of property calls they have taken in the last six months. Then tell them to write on one of the blank pieces of paper how many of those callers did not purchase from them, or that they are no longer actively working with. For example, if an agent took 20 calls from prospects over the last six months and sold only three of those leads' homes, and is still actively showing or corresponding with four other prospects, that agent should write the number 13 on the paper. Tell the group it is okay to make a reasonable guess. Have the group title this paper *Lost Opportunities*, then walk around the room and allow them to drop their papers into the wastebasket with the appropriate name.

Ask the group why some of the callers were lost opportunities. You will probably get several responses like *the caller was not qualified to purchase, needed to wait until the lease was up, was not serious, or other reasons that will probably be attributed to the potential buyers.*

Ask the following questions:

- Can we ever convert 100 percent of all property leads we come into contact with? *Of course the reality of life is that we cannot convert "everything" we come into contact with.*
- Can we "lose" more leads than we should? *The answer here is an overwhelming YES!*
- Why? *Some answers could be our attitude, our knowledge of the real estate business or knowledge of the inventory, and our tone of voice. All of these could play a major role in our not converting potential prospects.*

Step 3

Write the following list on the flip chart:

> Calls from:
>
> - Advertisements
> - Yard Signs
> - Internet Leads

Use the following categories to have the group brainstorm ways to work with each caller. For example, a call from a yard sign would indicate that the prospect has already driven by the outside of the property and is comfortable with the location and look of the home. This caller's primary concern is probably price. How could the agent approach this caller to get his or her name, phone number, and e-mail address if the price is too high? *Answer: Know the inventory for sale in this subdivision or particular area. Ask the caller "Were you interested in a home in this subdivision?"*

Use the same scenario for the other topics on your flip chart. Encourage the group to list ways to better serve the calls. Remind agents that if a caller is calling from an advertisement, for example, the agent should ask if the caller has other properties circled in competitors' ads the agent could check on for them. The key to being successful on each and every call is to communicate with the caller and build a relationship with him or her, so that you can ultimately set the appointment.

Step 4

After you discuss the previous examples, ask the group to help you develop a list of "Profitable Phone Tips." Go over the phone tips with your agents and list the suggestions on your flip chart. Promise to type and distribute these tips at your next meeting.

Step 5

Have agents pick up the second piece of paper that you provided them at the beginning of the meeting, and have them write the same number on it that was written on their first paper and discarded in the **Lost Opportunities** basket. Walk around the room again and have agents place their new papers in the other basket labeled **Future Profits**. As the agents place their papers in the basket, encourage them to make the next six months a more profitable experience, and to work on their phone techniques and ways to capitalize on each and every call they take.

Finish the Sales Meeting With This Quote:

> On the telephone: *"That's an amazing invention, but who would ever want to use one of them?"* Rutherford B. Hayes (1822–1893) Nineteenth president of the United States, ended support of carpetbag state governments in the south

ADDITIONAL NOTES TO COVER DURING MEETING

PROFESSIONAL DEVELOPMENT MEETING

14

Playing It Safe!

THEME: Playing It Safe!

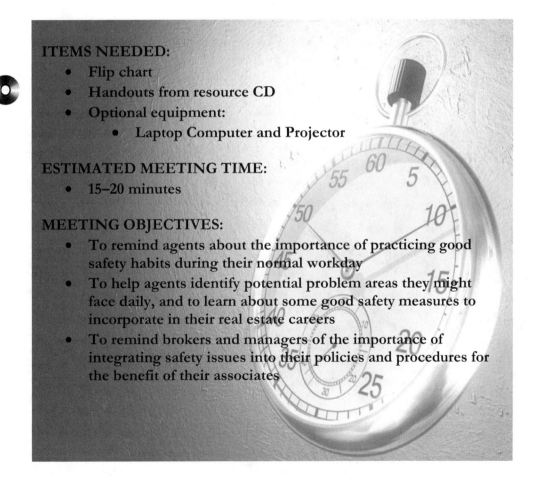

ITEMS NEEDED:
- Flip chart
- Handouts from resource CD
- Optional equipment:
  - Laptop Computer and Projector

ESTIMATED MEETING TIME:
- 15–20 minutes

MEETING OBJECTIVES:
- To remind agents about the importance of practicing good safety habits during their normal workday
- To help agents identify potential problem areas they might face daily, and to learn about some good safety measures to incorporate in their real estate careers
- To remind brokers and managers of the importance of integrating safety issues into their policies and procedures for the benefit of their associates

MEETING APPLICATION:

Step 1

Give out the following quiz for agents to complete:

Answer the following questions with either
Yes or *No*

1. _____ Do I know how to use the speed dial on my cell phone?
2. _____ Do I have 911 and other important phone numbers programmed into my first five speed dial numbers?
3. _____ Do I carry pepper spray in my automobile and with me when I am showing property to someone I do not know?
4. _____ Do I always let the receptionist or my broker/manager know where I am going when I leave the office?
5. _____ Do I always let the receptionist or my broker/manager know when I am planning to return when I leave the office?
6. _____ Do I always let the receptionist or my broker/manager know whom I am showing property to when I leave the office?
7. _____ Does my office have a copy of my automobile make, model, and license number on file?
8. _____ Does my office have a copy of my important contact numbers should an emergency arise during the day while I am at work?
9. _____ Does my office have a secret code word for high alert emergencies if I should call into the office, so the person answering knows I am in trouble?
10. _____ Do I usually hold my open houses by myself?
11. _____ When I hold an open house by myself, do I normally call into the office or check in with my family once an hour?
12. _____ Do I usually drive my own car when showing property to prospects?
13. _____ Does my office want me to make a copy of all prospective customers' driver's licenses or other forms of identification before leaving to show them properties?
14. _____ Do I normally walk behind buyers when showing them through a property?
15. _____ Is my home phone number listed on my business card?

Step 2

After agents have had a few minutes to finish the quiz, ask them how they scored. Explain to agents that if they had to place a "no" next to any of the questions, they might be at risk for an assault while practicing real estate.

Review the quiz with the group and ask for suggestions about the questions, then use their suggestions as well as the ones printed below:

1. _____ Do I know how to use the speed dial on my cell phone? *Knowing how to use your speed dial is critical! Not only may it help avoid an assault or attack, but it may also be invaluable in many other emergencies that could arise while you are working with clients or with your family. Encourage everyone to know how to use this feature before the end of business today!*

2. _____ Do I have 911 and other important phone numbers programmed into my first five speed dial numbers? *As noted above, this is an essential tool.*

3. _____ Do I carry pepper spray in my automobile and with me when I am showing property to someone I do not know? *Men and women should carry pepper spray in their cars and briefcases. In fact, have several cans available in your possession; in a purse, briefcase, automobile, and clipped to your key chain. Please note, some states or local municipalities may have laws that prohibit you to carry pepper spray. Always check on this before you keep pepper spray in your possession.*

4. _____ Do I always let the receptionist or my broker/manager know where I am going when I leave the office? *Included in this meeting agenda and on the CD is a sample Agent Itinerary Form provided by the Real Estate Safety Council. This is a good time to hand this form out to your agents and incorporate this into your daily policy.*

5. _____ Do I always let the receptionist or my broker/manager know when I am planning to return when I leave the office? *Reiterate the importance of the form you just handed out, and stress the need to make this mandatory for all agents.*

6. _____ Do I always let the receptionist or my broker/manager know who I am showing property to when I leave the office? *As in the previous two examples, make sure everyone agrees to adhere to this new policy.*

7. _____ Does my office have a copy of my automobile make, model, and license number on file? *This is a good time to pass out the handout for registering each agent's automobile make, model, and license number. Encourage everyone to have this completed once the meeting is over or by the end of this business day.*

8. _____ Does my office have a copy of my important contact numbers in case an emergency arises during the day while I am at work? *This is a good time to pass out the handout for registering each agent's important phone numbers and contact persons in case an emergency arises at work (if your office currently does not have this in place). Encourage everyone to have this completed once the meeting is over or by the end of this business day.*

9. _____ Does my office have a secret code word for high alert emergencies if I should call into the office so the person answering the phone knows I am in trouble? *Decide as a group what a good secret code would be for agents to use that would let the office know that this is an emergency alert. One good example from an article at the San Diego Board of REALTORS® web site by Lorrie Mowat, "REALTOR® Safety Tips" is to use the following statement if you are in trouble "Could you put the red file for 123 Smith St. on my desk?" The "red file" would indicate high alert, and the address given would represent the location where the agent is currently located and needs help.*

10. _____ Do I usually hold my open houses by myself? *Encourage agents to avoid holding open houses by themselves. Provide the following open house tips listed below:*

- Avoid holding the open house alone.

- Make sure you have a cell phone with you while attending the open house.

- Determine where all the escape routes are once you arrive at the open house.

- Park your car in front where you can easily drive away, rather than in the driveway where you may get blocked in.

- Check the backyard to discover if there is a fence and, if so, is there a gate and is it locked?

- Leave your business card with the date and time you arrived somewhere in the kitchen area. You might also suggest on the card whether there were visitors waiting before your arrival and whether you arrived alone.

- Keep the door locked until someone arrives.

- Keep a notebook with the make and model of the automobile (or at least a description) of each guest who attends your open house.

- Stay near an exit while the prospect looks at the home.

- Avoid walking in front of the prospect or going into a cellar or basement area with that person.

- Check in with your office or family often.

- Have the owners tell their neighbors about the open house and ask them to alert the police if they see anything that might seem unusual.

11. _____ When I hold an open house by myself, do I normally call into the office or check in with my family once an hour? *As noted above, this is a good practice when you hold open houses. A breakdown in communication could mean something is wrong and might alert a family member or the office to follow up on your situation.*

12. _____ Do I usually drive my own car when showing property to prospects? *There is nothing wrong with explaining to customers or clients whom you do not know that you will take your own car and that they can follow you. Use caution and good judgment before getting in anyone's automobile.*

13. _____ Does my office want me to make a copy of all prospective customers' driver's licenses or other forms of identification before leaving to show them properties? *Some agents may feel a little uncomfortable asking for this, but all you need to do is explain to the party that this is company policy and they should understand. Always require this if you feel a bit nervous, and always ask another agent to go with you if you have a bad feeling about a prospective client.*

14. _____ Do I normally walk behind buyers when showing them through a property? *Experts say that you should never take the lead when showing a property. Don't give a potential attacker the perfect opportunity to sneak up from behind you or push you into a room and shut the door.*

15. _____ Is my home phone number listed on my business card? *It is a good idea to have clients call your pager or voice mail rather than advertising your home phone number on your business cards. If you explain in advance to your prospects and clients how your voice mail or pager works and that you can immediately get back in touch with them, your business should not suffer.*

Step 3

Pose the following questions to the group:

- **Do you think most assaults are committed against female real estate agents?** The answer is "NO." Although women might be at greater risk of an attack while selling real estate, men can be at risk too. Mike Emert, a prominent and well-liked sales associate, was murdered in 2001 while showing a house. According to a study complied by The Louisiana REALTORS®, *REALTOR® Safety, Helpful Tips for Keeping safe on the Job*, between 1992 and 2001, 227 real estate practitioners were killed on the job nationwide. Many others were assaulted or robbed while out in the field.

- **Do you think most assaults occur during the first showing of a property?** Again, the answer is "NO." Mention to the group that, according to Robert Siciliano, personal safety trainer, speaker, and author, and his article from the Internet entitled *The Safety Minute: A Real Estate Agent's Guide To Taking A Minute For Safety*, "Con men are liars." Remind agents (especially the women in your organization) that many convicted attackers looked at homes the first time with their wives or girlfriends and children along. The assaults would often occur on a second or third showing, when the customer showed up alone.

- **What should you do if you were holding an open house by yourself, and a customer approached the home who made you feel uneasy?** One possible answer is to pretend to be involved in a telephone conversation and say something like, "Great, just bring the contract by here. I'll see you in couple of minutes." This will give the impression that someone is en route to the property and may discourage a possible attack.

Step 4

Ask the group if they can list any other points of information not covered during today's session. (You might check in advance with a local self-defense expert to see what the cost would be to offer a mini class to agents who might want to attend, and how many evenings or weekends the class would consist of.)

Close the meeting by reminding everyone that safety should always come first. Remind agents to work as teams and help each other out if a prospect makes one agent feel uneasy. Tell them not to sacrifice any standards, or place too much importance on keeping commission checks to themselves when it comes to personal safety. And, finally, follow up with the statement that someone needing quick cash for a drug problem or other issue could attack anyone from the office, male as well as female. *Everyone* needs to practice good safety tips!

Step 5

Hand out the pepper spray cans (if you chose to buy those for each agent present) or any other safety item you chose to buy.

Finish the Sales Meeting With This Quote:

"It is easy to be brave from a safe distance." Aesop (620–560 B.C.), Greek author of Aesop's Fables

ADDITIONAL NOTES TO COVER DURING MEETING

PROFESSIONAL
DEVELOPMENT
MEETING

15

Time Management

THEME: Managing Your Time More Effectively

ITEMS NEEDED:

- Flip chart
- Copies of newspapers (one for each group)
- Sales or real estate-related magazines, one for each group
- Book
- Daily calendar
- A map of your state
  Get this in advance and find a small community on the map at the other end of the state or as far as possible from your town. Take a highlighter or heavy black marker and draw a line from your community to the final destination by using roads you would have to travel to get there. Pin this map on the wall and then pin a large piece of white paper over the map so it's hidden. On this white paper hiding the map write the name of the small community that you have chosen.
- Handout from resource CD

ESTIMATED MEETING TIME:

- 10–15 minutes

MEETING OBJECTIVES:

- To help agents manage and plan their time better
- To encourage agents to evaluate which activities could be classified as "time wasters"
- To introduce agents to the concept of breaking their activities into smaller segments of time

MEETING APPLICATION:

Step 1

Write the following daily activities on the flip chart or, if you prefer, use the form (shown below) from the resource CD.

Description	Time Allotted
Meals (3 Times)	
Drive time to work	
Drive time from work	
Prospecting	
Filing and organization	
Phone calls	
Exercise	
Devotional or quiet time	
Quality time with spouse	
Quality time with children	
Showing property	
Listing property	
Time for me	
Television	
Miscellaneous	
Reading the local newspaper	
Reading books	

Have agents work on their own or in groups to complete the chart and estimate the time they spend on the various activities. If your group can come up with more time issues not listed, write those on your flip chart and encourage participants to include the newly added items to their lists. Once their lists are complete, have your agents transfer the time estimates to the daily calendar sheet that you provided them.

Step 2

Ask the following questions:

- What area consumes the most amount of your time each day?
- What area occupies the least amount of time in your daily schedule?
- Were there activities for which you allotted minimal or no time?
- What areas would you like to devote more time to each day?

Ask groups to talk about the last question among themselves, and discover ways to succeed in devoting time to their weak time-management areas. After a couple of minutes have the groups share areas of interest in their daily planning.

Step 3

Write the following phrase on a clean sheet of paper on your flip chart: **FIFTEEN-MINUTE RULE**. Explain to your group that the idea behind this thought is for them to take areas of their lives where they feel weak or nonproductive and begin carrying out a change in that area. For example, if many people listed exercise as an area that receives little or no attention, encourage those agents to begin devoting a 15-minute segment each day to exercise. This could include walking around the block, getting on a treadmill, or performing light aerobic exercise. (*Note:* Be sure to caution all of your agents to consult their doctors before performing any workout or exercise routine.) The same idea applies to reading: If there are agents who want to devote more time to reading, tell them to block off a 15-minute segment out of the day to read. Maybe there were agents who struggle with wanting more quality time with their spouses and children. If so, brainstorm ways and ideas for them to find more time for their loved ones. Many times reading a story to your children or taking a walk with your spouse and/or children can be very rewarding.

The bottom line is that everyone needs to do a better job of planning their daily, weekly, and monthly schedules. Encourage your group to set goals each day, and goals for their weekly and long-term planning. However, stress to your team that those goals should be in good balance; that is, they need to allocate time to spend with their families, loved ones, and also by themselves. Agents should also include exercise and education in their planning. By taking the time to plan what needs to be accomplished throughout the day, and by breaking those items into smaller segments (15 minutes or so) everyone should see a better picture of where they're going.

Step 4

Explain to the group that our lives and time are somewhat like taking a trip each day. Many of us do not know where our trip will lead us, and each day we start out without any road map of what we want to accomplish, or where we want to go.

Point to the white paper that has the name of the community you chose in your state. Ask the group if you were all leaving this room and would meet at the city chosen, how many of them could get there. Remove the blank paper from the wall to display the map of your state. Point out the small community miles away from your town and show the highlighted route from your town to the destination. Explain that, with a little time and preparation, reaching this destination would be a lot quicker and easier than just heading out with no road map or plan.

Share the following story:

"There was a story of three men who needed to travel from point A to point B. The major problem was that to get there each man would need to go down a steep hill, through a ravine, and then back up another large mountain. To make matters worse, there was a blinding snowstorm that each man would have to walk through during his trip. The first man said he would make the trek with no help and would walk his journey blindfolded. He set off for point B, never to be heard from again. The second man said that he would make the journey walking backwards. This man took off for the other mountain waving good-bye to everyone at the starting point walking backwards. The third colleague told the group that he would not walk blindfolded, nor backwards. He pulled a map out of his pocket and pointed to the star he had drawn on point B. 'I'm walking over there!' He left his destination and began his journey.

Who arrived first? The third man, of course. You see, the first man had no idea which way he was going. No map, no plans, 'Just blindfold me and send me out into the wilderness,' he said. 'I'll make it!' But he never did. The second man fared a little better and might eventually have made it to the other side, but he was constantly looking at his past and was so consumed with those issues that he was thrown off course and weaved and wagged his entire journey. But the third man knew from the beginning where his destination was and he walked straight toward it, and made it there first."

Step 5

Planning your day, week, or month can and will help you achieve more out of life. Finally, encourage agents to try the "15-Minute Rule." Devoting just a small time each day to areas of interest will make a big difference.

Finish the Sales Meeting With This Quote:

> *"The time to prepare isn't after you have been given the opportunity. It's long before that opportunity arises."* John Wooden, Former UCLA basketball coach

ADDITIONAL NOTES TO COVER DURING MEETING

TRACKING YOUR MEETINGS

One suggestion I have for brokers and managers who use my sales meeting book is to track your meetings each week. I have provided two tracking methods for this purpose. First, chart your meetings monthly to record those ideas that come about during and after the meetings. Sometimes you can get feedback during a meeting that will alert you to topics or areas of discussion your agents hunger for. Or, other times, you might try a particular teaching method, only to discover that it doesn't work well for your group. Keep track of these important notes with the Monthly Meeting Recap chart provided in this book. This can also be a good tool to use for legal issues that may arise in the future.

Second, track your meetings annually to provide a good mix of topics for your agents. By using the Annual Meeting Recap form provided in this book you can quickly glance back over a two- or three-month period and easily decide which topic areas need more attention. Trying to accomplish this feat in your head is simply not possible.

Good luck with your sales meetings, and I hope you find the book enjoyable and helpful. Most of all, I hope you're only "5 Minutes to a Great Real Estate Sales Meeting!"

John Mayfield

MONTHLY MEETING RECAP

Meeting Date	Meeting Description	Attendance Total	Positive Results	Negative Results

List any new ideas that came out of this month's meetings: _____

_____

ANNUAL MEETING RECAP

For Year of: _____

Place an "X" in the category that best describes your meeting. For example, if the title in Week 1 had a legal theme, place an "X" in the column marked "Legal." By charting your categories throughout the year, you will be able to assure that you give a good balance to the types of meetings you offer your agents.

Month	Meeting Title	Attendance Total	Motivational	Marketing	Prospecting	Legal	Professional Development
JANUARY							
Week 1							
Week 2							
Week 3							
Week 4							
Week 5							
FEBRUARY							
Week 1							
Week 2							
Week 3							
Week 4							
Week 5							
MARCH							
Week 1							
Week 2							
Week 3							
Week 4							
Week 5							
APRIL							
Week 1							
Week 2							
Week 3							
Week 4							
Week 5							
MAY							
Week 1							
Week 2							
Week 3							
Week 4							
Week 5							
JUNE							
Week 1							
Week 2							
Week 3							
Week 4							
Week 5							

Place an "X" in the category that best describes your meeting. For example, if the title in Week 1 had a legal theme, place an "X" in the column marked "Legal." By charting your categories throughout the year, you will be able to assure that you give a good balance to the types of meetings you offer your agents.

Month	Meeting Title	Attendance Total	Motivational	Marketing	Prospecting	Legal	Professional Development
JULY							
Week 1							
Week 2							
Week 3							
Week 4							
Week 5							
AUGUST							
Week 1							
Week 2							
Week 3							
Week 4							
Week 5							
SEPTEMBER							
Week 1							
Week 2							
Week 3							
Week 4							
Week 5							
OCTOBER							
Week 1							
Week 2							
Week 3							
Week 4							
Week 5							
NOVEMBER							
Week 1							
Week 2							
Week 3							
Week 4							
Week 5							
DECEMBER							
Week 1							
Week 2							
Week 3							
Week 4							
Week 5							

About the Author

John Mayfield received his real estate license at the age of 18 in 1978. John was one of the first sales associates in his board of REALTORS® to reach the Missouri Association of REALTORS® Million Dollar Club. John achieved this award during a time when interest rates were reaching record highs, and the average sales price in his marketplace was $25,000. John has been a practicing broker since 1981. He owns and operates three offices in Southeast Missouri, and manages more than 30 real estate agents. John has taught pre- and post-license real estate courses since 1988. He is the 2003 Technology Chairman for the Missouri Association of REALTORS®, and has served on many local and state committees and task forces for that REALTOR® organization. John has earned the ABR®, ABRM℠, GRI, e-PRO®, and CRB designations during his real estate tenure.

John is an avid real estate speaker and trainer. He has been a featured speaker at the Better Homes and Gardens Convention on three separate occasions, and has spoken to the Missouri Association of REALTORS® and the Springfield Board of REALTORS® conventions. He has also spoken to numerous boards of REALTORS® throughout Missouri and Arkansas, and currently serves on the Missouri Association of REALTORS® GRI staff. John has served as local board president twice, and has been awarded REALTOR-ASSOCIATE® of the Year and REALTOR® of the Year by his local board. John lives and breathes technology training and is always looking for new ways to make other real estate agents be more productive and save time.

You may contact John at JohnM@MayfieldRE.com, or visit his web site at http://www.EasyTechTips.com. You may also reach John by phone at 1-573-756-0077.

Index